JOURNEYS

Benchmark and Unit Tests

Grade 6

HOUGHTON MIFFLIN HARCOURT
School Publishers

"On the Move with Freddy Adu" by Marty Kaminsky from *Highlights for Children* magazine, June 2006. Text copyright © 2006 by Highlights for Children, Inc. Reprinted by Highlights for Children, Inc.

"Winter's End" by Pamela Love, illustrated by Julie Kim from *Spider* magazine, March 2006. Text copyright © 2006 by Carus Publishing Company. Illustrations copyright © 2006 by Julie Kim. Reprinted by permission of The Cricket Magazine Group, a division of Carus Publishing Company.

"Do You Want to Write a Poem?" by Myra Cohn Livingston. Text copyright © 1978 by Myra Cohn Livingston. Reprinted by permission of Marian Reiner Literary Agency.

"Keeping Cool with Crickets" by Lois Jacobson, illustrated by Karen Ritz in *Spider* magazine, June 2003. Text copyright © 1992 by Lois E. Jacobson. Illustrations copyright © 2003 by Karen Ritz. Reprinted by permission of the author and The Cricket Magazine Group, a division of Carus Publishing Company.

"Who Turned on the Faucet?" by Sarah E. Romanov, illustrated by Brian Biggs from *Spider* magazine, September 2005. Text copyright © 2005 by Sarah E. Romanov. Illustrations copyright © 2005 by Brian Biggs. Reprinted by permission from The Cricket Magazine Group, a division of Carus Publishing Company.

"Watch Out!" from *Watch Out for Clever Women!* by Joe Hayes, illustrated by Vicki Trego Hill. Text copyright © 1994 by Joe Hayes. Illustrations copyright © 1994 by Vicki Trego Hill. Reprinted by permission of Cinco Puntos Press, www.cincopuntos.com.

Printed in the U.S.A.

ISBN 10:   0-547-25718-X
ISBN 13:   978-0-547-25718-1

        8 9 10 0982 18 17 16 15 14 13 12 11

Contents

Reading

Read this selection. Then answer the questions that follow it.
Mark your answers on the Answer Document.

The Perfect Job

1   What do you think is the perfect job? I used to think it was one that would make me rich or famous, or both, but I recently came to realize that the best occupation is one that suits an individual perfectly. I learned this from my Uncle Charles, whose job fits him like a glove.

2   Charles is an Animal Control Officer (ACO) for the municipality of Hartford, the town where I live, too. My father says jokingly that his brother likes animals better than people, and I share my father's opinion. He says that even as a kid Charles had a reputation for rescuing stray dogs, helping wounded chickadees, and plucking stranded cats from high branches. Today Charles can be recognized by his fascinating facial hair—a curly beard and handlebar mustache. He's content to live alone, companioned by the various critters that pass through his care.

3   One April day my teachers had a conference to attend, and since my folks both work, I had permission to spend the day with Uncle Charles. Soon after I arrived at his farmhouse, the phone rang and he switched on the speakerphone so I could hear his call. A distraught-sounding woman was on the line. "There's an animal in the woods behind my house," the woman quavered, "and it's howling over and over. The noise kept me awake all last night. Please come fetch the poor thing."

4   "Be right over," Charles replied, jotting down her address on an old envelope. We hopped into his old red pickup truck and took off.

5   The woman lived on Upton Road, a rutted country lane lined with immense pines that created a gloomy shade, even though it was midday. When we pulled into the driveway at a mailbox numbered 458, a petite woman emerged from a small house wearing work clothes, a cap for shade from the sun, and muddy boots. She directed us toward the woods but admitted she was reluctant to go with us. "I think it's just a dog, but I was bitten by a dog when I was a child," she explained, "and I just don't want to take a chance."

6   We tromped through the nettles and sumac behind the house till we found a path into the woods. Suddenly we heard a pitiful yowl. "Stand back," my uncle commanded. I stayed a short distance behind him, but kept craning my neck around my uncle's frame. As we got closer, I saw a long, low-slung dog wearing a faded purple collar; the metal ring that holds the tags hung empty. She was cowering close to the ground, clearly more afraid of us than we were of her. She had long droopy ears, and her eyes, too, were droopy. She looked miserable.

7   My uncle whispered, "It's okay, girl," and she trembled but let him clip a leash to her collar and lead her to the truck. When he opened the back door, she hopped right in.

8   As we drove, I spoke soothingly to the dog, and she seemed to grow more comfortable with us. Back in my uncle's kitchen, he scrunched some blankets into a bed for her and put down fresh water and a dish of kibble. She gobbled the food and slurped the water, then flopped on the blankets and closed her droopy eyes. My uncle clomped into the kitchen and booted up his old computer.

9   "LOST DOG HARTFORD BASSET," he typed into the search engine. The computer hummed through the slow dial-up process until the classified ads for the local newspaper appeared, and my uncle began to scroll. There it was, the third ad down: a lost basset hound with a purple collar from Sumner, a neighboring town.

10   He called the phone number immediately, and when a man answered, my uncle introduced himself and passed on the good news. "They've found Happy!" I heard the man call to someone else. "We'll be right over, okay?" After my uncle gave him directions, the man was in such a hurry to hang up that he dropped the phone three times!

GO ON

Name _____ Date _____

11   It wasn't long before a red convertible squealed into the driveway and a father and his son emerged. When Happy saw them, there was certainly no doubt that this was her family. The son got down on his hands and knees, laughing, hugging, and letting Happy jump, slobber, squirm, and wag as much as she wanted.

12   "We don't know how to thank you," the father confided to my uncle, his voice cracking some. "We've been sick with worry, and I must admit we feared the worst." There were tears in his eyes, but my uncle was grinning.

13   In that moment I understood that my Uncle Charles had the perfect occupation.

1   The reader can conclude that Happy's owners—

A   grew up in Hartford

B   liked to drive fast cars

C   gave up on finding the dog

D   were desperate to find the dog

2   What does the reader learn about Uncle Charles?

F   He is unhappy.

G   He does not get along well with people.

H   He has no children of his own.

J   He enjoys the company of animals.

3   The narrator compares Uncle Charles's job to—

A   the work of a detective

B   a close fitting glove

C   an Animal Control Officer

D   the perfect occupation

4   Uncle Charles has the narrator stand back because Uncle Charles—

F   wants credit for finding the dog

G   has a leash for the dog

H   wants to protect the narrator

J   knows that danger lies ahead

5   The narrator thinks Uncle Charles's job is perfect because Uncle Charles—

A   drives an old truck

B   is not wealthy

C   works outdoors

D   makes people happy

GO ON

Name _____   Date _____

**Read this selection. Then answer the questions that follow it.
Mark your answers on the Answer Document.**

On the Move with Freddy Adu

by Marty Kaminsky

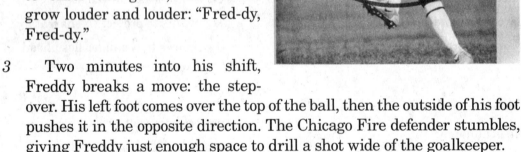

1   The crowd in R.F.K. Stadium anxiously scans the sideline. As Washington's D.C. United soccer team takes on the Chicago Fire, excited fans are looking for Freddy Adu (uh-DOO). "Where's Freddy?" they call from their seats.

2   Finally, 16-year-old Freddy Adu pulls off his warm-up suit. The crowd roars. As Freddy jogs up and down the sideline, waiting to enter the game, the chants grow louder and louder: "Fred-dy, Fred-dy."

3   Two minutes into his shift, Freddy breaks a move: the step-over. His left foot comes over the top of the ball, then the outside of his foot pushes it in the opposite direction. The Chicago Fire defender stumbles, giving Freddy just enough space to drill a shot wide of the goalkeeper.

4   The crowd is on its feet, oohing and aahing at the near miss. Freddy does not score this time, but it is plain for all to see: there are many goals to come in the future of this American soccer phenomenon.

5   At the age of 14, when most kids are starting eighth or ninth grade, Freddy signed the largest contract ever with Major League Soccer, the American men's professional league. A flood of stories about him immediately appeared in magazines and newspapers.

6   "It's pretty hard not to get caught up in all of it," Freddy admits. "But my friends and family remind me of what is most important and keep me grounded."

7   In 1997, Freddy's family moved from Ghana, West Africa, to Mrs. Adu's brother's house in the United States so that Freddy and his brother, Fro, could get a better education.

8   Freddy now lives with his mother and brother in Rockville, Maryland, not far from the home field of his team, D.C. United.

9   Although most sports stars hire assistants to handle their household chores, Freddy's mom treats Freddy like any other 16-year-old. "My mom makes me do chores, like the dishes, same as before," Freddy laments. "I don't like it, but I do it."

10 In Ghana, kids were constantly knocking on Freddy's door to ask him to play soccer. From age two on, Freddy played barefoot games on sandy fields.

11 "I did not go one day without soccer," Freddy recalls. "There were no coaches, so it was just kicking and learning on your own."

12 As he got older, Freddy began playing in games with boys twice his age and in scrimmages against men.

13 Soon after arriving in America at the age of eight, Freddy was discovered by a schoolmate's dad, a youth-soccer coach. Freddy joined the coach's all-star team.

14 When Freddy was 10, the team traveled to an international tournament in Italy, where Freddy scored four goals in five games and

Name _____ Date _____

won the Most Valuable Player award. An Italian professional league offered Freddy a contract at that time, but Mrs. Adu turned it down. Freddy explains, "I was only 10. . . . As usual, she was looking out for my well-being in the long run."

15   When Freddy returned to the United States, Mrs. Adu let him attend a sports boarding school in Florida that is run by the U.S. Soccer Federation. Freddy completed all his course requirements and finished high school when he was 14.

16   By then, Freddy had drawn the interest of some of the soccer world's most important people. Bruce Arena, coach of the USA men's national team, noted, "He's strong, he's quick, he's agile. He's got good balance, and he's got great vision. . . . This player may be our first superstar."

17   Although teams from around the world clamored for Freddy's attention, Freddy decided to play in the United States. He wanted to live as normal a teenage life as possible. "I like to do lots of things that other teenagers do," Freddy says. "One of the hardest things for me is that soccer is my work, so I don't have a normal teenage life. I travel around a lot and hang out with guys much older than me who have different interests."

18   It might be easy for a 16-year-old to let it go to his head when fans chant his name and beg for autographs, but Freddy has learned a lot in his two years with D.C. United. "I am just one person on a team—I'm not the whole team," he explains. "And this is about more than soccer—it is about how you carry yourself, how you behave, and how much you respect others."

6 Mrs. Adu moved her family to the United States to—

   F be closer to her brother

   G let Freddy play soccer

   H provide a better education for her sons

   J have the family closer to the D.C United home field

7 After reading the final quote from Freddy, which of the following best describes him?

   A Arrogant

   B Meek

   C Ambitious

   D Humble

8 Which sentence presents a main idea of this passage?

   F Although Freddy Adu is a star athlete, he is also a regular teenage boy.

   G Being a star athlete has an upside and a downside.

   H Soccer is becoming more popular in America thanks to Freddy Adu.

   J In order to succeed as a professional athlete, it is best to start young.

9 The author's attitude toward Freddy Adu is—

   A skeptical

   B concerned

   C admiring

   D fanatical

10 Which is the best paraphrase of this sentence from the passage?

"Freddy does not score this time, but it is plain for all to see: there are many goals to come in the future of this American soccer phenomenon."

   F Even though Freddy doesn't score, he will be a great player.

   G Freddy didn't score, and he won't in the future either.

   H The whole crowd expected him to make a goal.

   J Freddy will need more practice and experience to succeed.

Read this selection. Then answer the questions that follow it.
Mark your answers on the Answer Document.

Everything You Wanted To Know About Pencils

1   The story of pencils begins about 500 years ago in the Cumberland Hills of England. One day, after a violent storm, a group of shepherds went out to check their sheep. Several trees had blown over, exposing a grey-black glistening substance. Like coal, it quickly stained their fingers, but unlike coal, it would not burn. They did, however, discover that the new substance was excellent for marking the sheep! They called the substance black lead.

2   Eventually, someone developed a holder for black lead. A piece of wood was hollowed out and a piece of black lead was placed inside. The wood could then be scraped away as the writing material was used. Later, people started using a different method to make pencils. Two pieces of planed and smoothed wood were glued around a narrow stick of black lead. This technique is still used today. About the same time, a Swedish chemist learned that black lead, like its upscale cousin, the diamond, was a form of carbon. He renamed black lead *graphite*, which comes from a Greek word meaning "to write."

3   In the early nineteenth century, most pencils sold in the United States were imported from Europe. Soon, however, pencil factories started to open. Early pencils were unpainted, to show off their high quality wood. Most pencils were made from Eastern Red Cedar, a strong splinter-resistant wood that grows in the eastern United States.

4   As more and more pencils were made and sold, competition became strong and advertising became essential. The biggest and best pencil makers painted their pencils yellow to show that they used Chinese graphite, the finest in the

GO ON ▶

world. In China, yellow is the color of royalty and respect, so pencil makers chose yellow for their highest-quality products. Today, seventy-five percent of the pencils sold in the United States are yellow.

5   Today's pencils are made with more than just graphite. Graphite is combined with clay and inserted into a wooden casing. This combination will probably be used throughout the next centuries.

Pencil Facts

- Most pencils are hexagonal, which is comfortable to hold, and it means the pencils won't roll off their desks.

- Pencils work in space because they do not use gravity, unlike most pens.

- Most U.S. pencils have erasers, but most European pencils do not.

- A typical pencil can write 45,000 words.

- A typical pencil can draw a line 35 miles long!

- Pencils are labeled according to the hardness of their graphite. In the United States, a #2 is medium, which is preferred during standardized tests.

---

11 What is the main idea of the first paragraph?

   A Pencils were invented in England about 500 years ago.

   B About 500 years ago, English shepherds found black lead.

   C About 500 years ago, pencils were used to mark sheep.

   D Black lead stains people's skin but does not burn.

12 Most pencils are yellow to—

   F indicate that they come from China

   G make them easy to see in a messy drawer

   H make them easier for the user to hold

   J suggest that they are high quality

13 Which sentence is the best summary of the last paragraph?

   A Modern pencils combine graphite, clay, and wood.

   B Modern pencils last much longer than their earlier versions.

   C Pencils are the product of competition and advertising.

   D Pencils are losing popularity to pens and computers.

14 How are most American pencils different from most European pencils?

   F Most American pencils can write or draw longer than most European ones.

   G Most American pencils use graphite; most European pencils use lead.

   H Most American pencils have erasers; most European pencils do not.

   J Most American pencils use friction; most European pencils use gravity.

15 What kind of graphic feature is "Pencil Facts"?

   A A bar graph

   B A timeline

   C A bulleted list

   D A diagram

GO ON

10

Read this selection. Then answer the questions that follow it.
Mark your answers on the Answer Document.

California Beach

I.

Horns honk in smoggy rush hour traffic.
A big man hoses down a sidewalk
while another empties trash cans from the day before.
Early morning joggers pant, sweat, stare.
Seagulls scavenge yesterday's fries as moms push babies in strollers,
and somewhere a boom box thumps
as the sky turns from rosy pink to orange to yellow to red to turquoise,
thick and perfect as paint.
The waves lick the sand gently as the tide and the people flow in.

II.

People on blankets soak up sun, while
the smell of coconut oil floats on the breeze like samba music.
Artists sell watercolors of the wooden pier
while surfers wait in the doldrums for waves,
toddlers wail, sleepy, couples walk hand in hand.
A steel drum clangs and teenagers dance,
seagulls beg for potato chips,
the sun rises high.
"Burritos!" shouts a vendor.
Inline skates, bicycles, skateboards, scooters.
"Wait up!" yells a girl on a pink tricycle.
The tide retreats, leaving the clamor behind.

Name _____ Date _____

III.
Palm trees are silhouettes against fire as the sun sinks.
Families giggle, chasing beach balls in the sand
as old men play chess in the shade.
Artists pack their wares, bid goodnight,
and seagulls dine on pizza crusts as seaweed dries, clouds drift, breezes
whisper, break-dancers spin. Children swing so high
their sandals touch the violet clouds, the sun
now an ember, glowing red, pink, then purple.
The tide rises, always moving,
always changing, always the same.

GO ON ▶

16 Which detail from the third verse shows that evening is approaching?

F Old men play chess

G The clouds are violet

H The sun/now an ember

J Seagulls eat pizza crusts

17 One way the poet marks the passing of time is by—

A showing the rise and fall of the tide

B referring to the noises heard at midday

C describing people of many different ages

D contrasting dark trees against the sunset

18 What repeated image ties the three verses together?

F Alternating long and short lines

G Showing different family activities

H The sounds of cars on the beach

J The feeding patterns of seagulls

19 The last line of the first verse compares the—

A incoming tide and the people arriving

B waves on the beach and an animal

C movement of the waves and the rising tide

D waves and a kind, gentle person

20 Which image from the poem is an example of personification?

F Sandals touch the violet clouds

G Waves lick the sand

H Steel drum clangs

J Old men play chess

21 The literary element most evident in "California Beach" is—

A plot

B setting

C characters

D theme

GO ON

Read this selection. Then answer the questions that follow it.
Mark your answers on the Answer Document.

"Evacuate!"

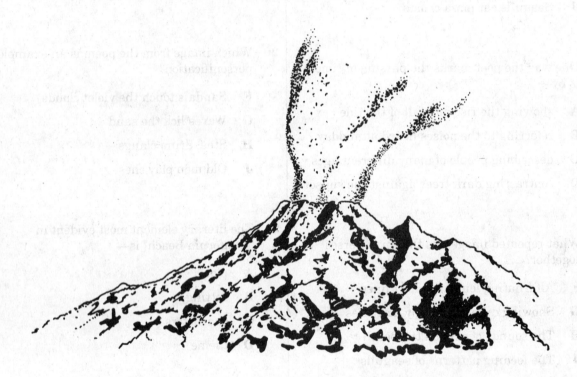

1   Emil and his family live thirty-five kilometers north of Mount Merapi, an active volcano in Central Java in Indonesia, on land that his great-great-great-grandparents once farmed. They are as firmly planted there as the rice that returns every year to their fields.

2   For weeks now, the family has heard Merapi, which means mountain of fire, rumbling and grumbling like an underground giant. Lava flows down the north side of Mount Merapi. Hot ash and steam spew from the top. Already, gas clouds have nearly choked one village, and ash has covered another with a thick, gray blanket.

3   "This morning we raised the status of Merapi to red, which is the top alert," said the head of the Center for Vulcanologic Research. "Since the mountain is in a state of constant lava flow, every resident within forty kilometers has been ordered to evacuate."

4   After their evening meal of *nasi goreng*, a traditional meal of rice, egg, and chicken, Emil's father and uncle sit and discuss the news. Usually, Emil would go with his brother and two sisters to play badminton outside. Tonight, he wants to hear what the men say, so he crouches behind a chair to avoid notice.

5   Emil's father is a tall, thin man, with a soft voice. He sits on one side of the room and calmly explains that they must stay. He argues that all they own in both houses, including the livestock, will be in danger, not just from the volcano but also from looters. He says that the crops might be saved if they stay, but they will certainly die if the family leaves. Without the crops, he says, the two families will have nothing to eat when they return. Emil's father reminds his brother that the government has evacuated the people before and the lava did not reach them.

6   His older brother, a big man with a huge black beard and a gruff voice, answers that they must leave. The military trucks will come and make them leave. He says the military has had to use force in some of the villages, and there is fear in his throat as he talks. "Every time the mountain erupts, people suffer," he says, "and it is always the foolish people who decide to stay."

7   Emil can see his father tremble as he looks out at the rice paddies he has tended since he was a boy. Suddenly, he notices his son crouching behind the chair. "Go outside and play with the others," he barks. Emil obeys him, as he always does.

8   The next morning, the children rise to find that all the families' belongings have been packed. In the distance, Merapi moans and groans, and the sky to the south is dark with ash and smoke. After the chores are complete, the two families will head north.

Name _____   Date _____

22 Which statement describes Emil's point of view in the story?

   F   Emil is an unconcerned observer.

   G   Emil directs the events of the story.

   H   Emil is the narrator of the story.

   J   Emil is both a participant and an observer.

23 What is Emil's father's argument for staying?

   A   If the families leave, they will certainly die, as there will be nothing to eat when they return; and, at any rate, the government is not always right.

   B   The volcano is far away, and it is only posing a risk to towns and villages.

   C   If the families leave, they will risk losing their animals and crops; and, at any rate, the government has unnecessarily evacuated people before.

   D   The families must remain at home to look after their animals and crops, and they should never give in to the government.

24 Mount Merapi symbolizes—

   F   a force of evil and destruction

   G   the islands of Indonesia

   H   the unpredictable force of nature

   J   volcanoes all over the world

25 In paragraph 4, Emil eavesdrops on the men because he—

   A   likes to be included with the grown-ups

   B   knows their discussion will be important

   C   is too nervous to play badminton

   D   wants to be part of the decision

26 Which description from the story uses a simile?

   F   *the sky to the south is dark with ash and smoke*

   G   *His older brother, a big man with a huge black beard*

   H   *every resident within forty kilometers*

   J   *grumbling like an underground giant*

27 In paragraph 7, Emil's father trembles. The reader can infer that Emil's father—

   A   is worried that Emil will leave

   B   is angry at his brother for disagreeing with him

   C   has realized that the family must evacuate

   D   has noticed Emil crouching behind a chair

Name _____ Date _____

**Read this selection. Then answer the questions that follow it.
Mark your answers on the Answer Document.**

Spend or Save!

1   Many people are paid either weekly or monthly, because they have a job, or because they get an allowance. These people have expenses, too, or things that cost them money, and the earned money can help them take care of those expenses.

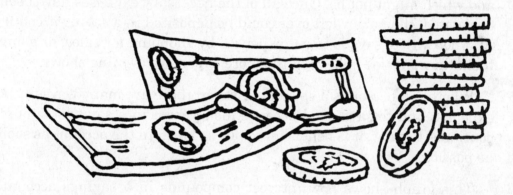

The Choice

2   One person may choose to spend the money he or she earns immediately. This person may purchase triple fudge brownies, newly released video games, or perhaps tickets to a popular movie, and soon, this person may be out of funds, having spent all that hard earned money. A different person may choose not to spend the money right away, but save it, stashing the money in his or her mattress, or investing it in a bank.

Why Save?

3   Saving is actually easy to do, especially if the money is deposited into a savings account. The savings account is kept by the bank, and the money in the account earns interest. Interest is earned based on the amount of money in the account, which is called the balance. An interest rate of three percent earns three cents for every dollar kept in the account. The longer the money is kept in the account, the more interest that is earned, which is added to the existing balance. Soon the interest becomes part of a new balance and earns interest. This

phenomenon is called compound interest. Money left for long periods of time in a bank earns money, almost as though it gets its own allowance!

How to Save

4   There are several ways to increase the amount of money available to put in the bank. One is to take an amount of money from a paycheck or allowance and put it in the bank first, before spending any money. The second is to create a plan, or budget, by keeping a money diary, writing down all the money earned and all the money spent on expenses. Looking at the diary can help determine which expenses are necessary and which might not be. Once all of the necessary expenses have been calculated, the money left over could be deposited in a saving account. Another way to save is to cut expenses by shopping for sales, or going to matinee movies instead of the more expensive evening shows.

5   Whether a person is a spender or saver, there are many ways to cut expenses and to save. And because money kept in a savings account continues to grow, it is beneficial to put as much in the account as soon as possible.

6   This graph shows how interest compounds in a savings account. The owner of the account started with $50 and adds $5 every year.

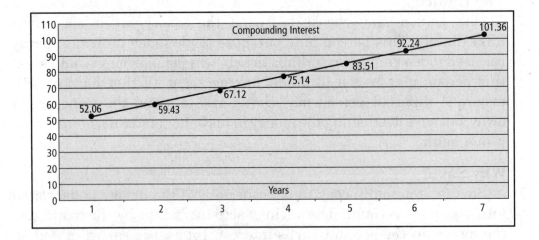

28 Around what two contrasting ideas is this article organized?

F Saving money in a bank or saving it at home

G Buying freely or saving for the future

H Cutting expenses or budgeting funds

J A bank that pays interest or a bank that does not

29 The purpose of this article is to—

A entertain readers with stories about money

B encourage readers to save money

C give information about interest rates at various banks

D explain how savings and checking accounts are different

30 Which is the best paraphrase of this sentence from the passage?

"Money left for long periods of time in a bank earns money, almost as though it gets it own allowance!"

F Getting an allowance is better than getting a paycheck.

G Money in a savings account is more difficult to spend than cash.

H Keeping money in a bank for many months earns more money.

J Money will earn interest at a higher rate if it is in a bank.

31 Which sentence describes the "saving" and "spending" advice in this article?

A More advice is about spending than saving.

B More advice is about saving than spending.

C The advice about spending and saving is equal and balanced.

D There is no advice about spending or saving.

32 The graph supports the argument presented in the passage by showing that—

F people do not earn money in savings accounts

G people can earn money in savings accounts

H spending will increase over time

J future prices will be higher

BE SURE TO MARK YOUR ANSWERS ON THE ANSWER DOCUMENT.

Writing: Revising and Editing

> Read the introduction and the passage that follows it. Then read each
> question. Mark your answers on the Answer Document.

*Melissa wrote this report about the American Museum of Natural History.
She would like you to read it and think about changes she needs to make.
Then answer the questions that follow.*

The American Museum of Natural History

(1) If you go to New York City, plan on visiting the American Museum
of Natural History. (2) You may have seen the museum in a popular
fictional movie about what happens to the exhibits at night. (3) As exciting
as the museum looks in the movie, it is even more exciting in real life.

(4) To enter the museum, you walk up several concrete stairs. (5) When
you step inside, a very, very big, long-necked dinosaur skeleton greets you.
(6) Just ahead are 28 mammal dioramas featuring a herd of life-sized
elephants and other African mammals.

(7) Go down a level to the first floor and you will find a 94-foot-long blue
whale in the Milstein Hall of Ocean Life. (8) This amazing cite is suspended
from the ceiling high above you. (9) In this big Hall, visitors admire not only
the blue whale, but also marine animals and plants of all shapes and sizes.

(10) The Arthur Ross Hall of Meteorites is also located on the first floor. (11) Here you will find moon rocks. (12) You will find other interesting items from space, including the Cape York Meteorite, the world's largest meteorite in a museum. (13) It weighs an astounding 34 tons. (14) If you enjoy learning about space, be sure to visit the museum's Rose Center for Earth and Space. (15) It is home to a planetarium and numerous exhibits about the stars and planets.

(16) The museum is open almost every day from 10 A.M. to 5:45 P.M.

(17) There is so much to see, do, and learn at the museum a knowledgeable tour guide can help you discover all the museum has to offer.

---

1 What change should be made in sentence 5?

  A Delete the comma after *inside*

  B Change *very, very big* to **gigantic**

  C Change *dinosaur* to **Dinosaur**

  D Change *greets* to **greeted**

2 Which sentence could BEST follow sentence 6?

  F The elephant is the largest living land mammal.

  G Each year, millions of people visit the museum.

  H They are so life-like that you can practically smell them!

  J The American Museum of Natural History has changing exhibits.

3 What change should be made in sentence 8?

  A Change *amazing* to **amazed**

  B Change *cite* to **sight**

  C Change *suspended* to **suspends**

  D Insert a comma after *above*

4 What change should be made in sentence 9?

  F Change *Hall* to **hall**

  G Delete the comma after *whale*

  H Change *marine* to **Marine**

  J Change the period to a question mark

GO ON

5   What is the BEST way to combine sentences 11 and 12?

   A   Here you will find moon rocks and other interesting items from space, including the Cape York Meteorite, the world's largest meteorite in a museum.

   B   Here you will find moon rocks and you will find other interesting items from space, including the Cape York Meteorite, the world's largest meteorite in a museum.

   C   Here you will find moon rocks and other interesting items from space, it is the world's largest meteorite in a museum including the Cape York Meteorite.

   D   Here you will find moon rocks and items from space that are interesting, including you will find the Cape York Meteorite, the world's largest meteorite in a museum.

6   What change should be made in sentence 13?

   F   Change *It* to **Its**

   G   Change *weighs* to **ways**

   H   Change *tons* to **ton**

   J   Change the period to an exclamation point

7   What is the BEST way to revise sentence 17?

   A   There is so much to see, do, and learn at the museum a knowledgeable tour guide. Can help you discover all the museum has to offer.

   B   There is so much to see, do, and learn at the museum because knowledgeable tour guide can help you discover all the museum has to offer.

   C   There is so much to see, do, and learn at the museum a knowledgeable tour guide can help you discover.

   D   There is so much to see, do, and learn at the museum. A knowledgeable tour guide can help you discover all the museum has to offer.

GO ON

> **Read the introduction and the passage that follows it. Then read each question. Mark your answers on the Answer Document.**

Evan wrote a story about how he overcame a fear. He wants you to help him revise and edit the story. Read Evan's story and think about the changes you would make. Then answer the questions that follow.

Testing the Water

(1) Many people are afraid of something. (2) For example, they might have a phobia of big spiders or chaotic thunderstorms. (3) These specific fears do not apply to me. (4) I have a pet tarantula named "Buddy," and I happen to enjoy a sudden flash of lightning and an earsplitting clap of thunder. (5) However, I did have one fear. (6) As ridiculous as it might sound, throughout my entire life I've been absolutely terrified of water.

(7) My friends enjoy swimming. (8) Most members of my family enjoy swimming. (9) On Saturdayes, whenever the weather got warm, my friends and family members would try to get me to swim at the local swimming pool with them. (10) Of course, I always had some excuse about why I couldn't go, and sometimes I refused their invitations outright. (11) I usually regretted this decision, but what else could I do.

GO ON

(12) This summer I signed up for swimming lessons at the Kilgore Community center. (13) I've done so each summer in the past, but I always cancelled at the last minute. (14) This year I forced myself to show up on the first day.

(15) Fortunately, I had a well-trained instructor. (16) Patient and understanding. (17) My teacher knew just what to say and how far to nudge me before I became uncomfortable. (18) By the end of the first day, I was already submerging my face in the water. (19) By the end of the week, I was actually swimming!

(20) Now my friends and family do not have to coxe me to go to the pool with them. (21) I'm usually the one trying to get them to go. (22) I am also the first one in the water!

---

8 What is the BEST way to combine sentences 7 and 8?

F My friends enjoy swimming and members of my family mostly enjoy swimming, too.

G My friends enjoy swimming most members of my family enjoy swimming, too.

H My friends and most members of my family enjoy swimming.

J My friends enjoy swimming and my family members enjoy swimming most.

9 What change should be made in sentence 9?

A Change *Saturdayes* to **Saturdays**

B Delete the comma after *warm*

C Change *swim* to **swims**

D Change *local swimming pool* to **Local Swimming Pool**

GO ON

10 What change should be made in sentence 11?

   F Change *regretted* to **regret**

   G Change *decision* to **decisions**

   H Change *do* to **did**

   J Change the period to a question mark

11 What change should be made in sentence 12?

   A Change *signed* to **sign**

   B Change *lessons* to **lessones**

   C Change *center* to **Center**

   D Change the period to an exclamation point

12 Which sentence could BEST be added after sentence 14?

   F Swimming looks like a lot of fun, but it frightens me.

   G My older brother learned to swim at the community center.

   H Swimming lessons are offered in sessions that run for four weeks.

   J I was so nervous that my heart was racing and my palms were sweating.

13 What is the BEST way to combine sentences 16 and 17?

   A My teacher, patient and understanding, knew just what to say and how far to nudge me before I became uncomfortable.

   B Patient and understanding, knowing just what to say and how far to nudge me before I became uncomfortable was my teacher.

   C Before I became uncomfortable, my teacher became patient and understanding, knowing just what to say and how far to nudge.

   D Patient and understanding my teacher knew just what to say, and how far to nudge me, before I became uncomfortable.

14 What change should be made in sentence 20?

   F Insert a comma after *family*

   G Change *coxe* to **coax**

   H Change *go* to **goes**

   J Change *pool* to **Pool**

> **Read the introduction and the passage that follows it. Then read each question. Mark your answers on the Answer Document.**

Kenzie had to write a book report for her class. She wants you to read her paper and help correct it. After you read the book report, answer the questions that follow.

A Book Worth Reading

(1) The writer Avery Fisher has done it again? (2) You will want to read her latest book, <u>On the Job</u>, over and over. (3) In it, twelve-year-old Meagan devotes a weekend to Babysitting classes to learn the ins and outs of caring for children. (4) By the end of the following week, her neighbor hires her to go with the family on a camping trip and help the mother with her three young childrens.

(5) The camping trip begins well, and Meagan is enjoying herself and her job. (6) On a walk in the woods with the family, Meagans' relaxation vanishes when the two-year old falls down and gets a cut. (7) At first, Meagan panics, but she quickly recovers and remembers her training. (8) She takes the first aid kit out of her backpack, puts on gloves, and begins cleansing the cut and covering it with a bandage while the mother watches.

(9) Readers will enjoy the action in the book. (10) They will sympathize with the struggles Meagan faces. (11) Readers will sympathize with the struggles Meagan overcomes. (12) Young babysitters will realize that the job involves more than just entertaining it is a lot of work and responsibility. (13) With her latest book, Avery Fisher sends a message in a great, great way!

15 What change, if any, should be made in sentence 1?

- **A** Change *writer* to **Writer**
- **B** Insert a comma after *Fisher*
- **C** Change the question mark to an exclamation point
- **D** Make no change

16 What change should be made in sentence 3?

- **F** Change *devotes* to **deavotes**
- **G** Change *Babysitting* to **babysitting**
- **H** Change *learn to* **learning**
- **J** Insert a comma after *caring*

17 What change should be made in sentence 4?

- **A** Delete the comma after *week*
- **B** Change *hires* to **hired**
- **C** Change *mother* to **Mother**
- **D** Change *childrens* to **children**

18 What change should be made in sentence 6?

- **F** Change *Meagans'* to **Meagan's**
- **G** Change *vanishes* to **vanyshes**
- **H** Insert a period after *down*
- **J** Change *gets* to **got**

19 What is the BEST way to combine sentences 10 and 11?

- **A** They will sympathize with the struggles Meagan faces and overcomes.
- **B** They will sympathize with the struggles she overcomes and Meagan faces.
- **C** They will sympathize with the struggles and overcomes Meagan faces.
- **D** They will sympathize with Meagan and struggles and readers will sympathize with the struggles she overcomes.

20 What is the BEST way to rewrite the ideas in sentence 12?

F Young babysitters will realize that the job involves more than just entertaining, work, and responsibility.

G Young babysitters will realize that the job involves more than just entertaining. A lot of work and responsibility.

H Young babysitters will realize. The job involves more than just entertaining it is a lot of work and responsibility.

J Young babysitters will realize that the job involves more than just entertaining. It is a lot of work and responsibility.

21 What change should be made in sentence 13?

A Change *book* to **Book**

B Change *sends* to **sent**

C Insert a comma after *message*

D Change *great, great* to **wonderful**

BE SURE TO MARK YOUR ANSWERS ON THE ANSWER DOCUMENT.

STOP

Name _____ Date _____

Writing: Written Composition

> Write a fictional narrative about a character who overcomes a challenge.

Use a separate sheet of paper to plan your composition. Then write your composition on the lined pages that follow.

The information in the box below will help you remember what you should think about when you write your composition.

REMEMBER—YOU SHOULD

❑ write about a character who overcomes a challenge

❑ have a clear beginning, middle, and ending

❑ introduce the characters and the setting in the beginning

❑ include a conflict and climax and conclude with a satisfying resolution of the conflict

❑ include details and dialogue that bring the story to life

❑ try to use correct spelling, capitalization, punctuation, grammar and sentences

---

Name _____ Date _____

_____

_____

_____

_____

_____

_____

_____

_____

_____

_____

_____

_____

_____

_____

_____

Name _____ Date _____

_____

_____

_____

_____

_____

_____

_____

_____

_____

_____

_____

_____

_____

Reading

> **Read this selection. Then answer the questions that follow it.**
> **Mark your answers on the Answer Document.**

Kids Making a Difference

1   All around the country, the power of older kids is making an impact. These students are showing they have a valuable talent for inspiring younger children to do their best.

Tutors in Seattle

2   Young children sometimes become frustrated by their homework. In one Seattle after-school program, student tutors come to the rescue. They make learning into a game that kids enjoy. They also read to the children and help them with crafts when their homework is done. The younger students are happy to get help with their homework. They are even happier to get the attention of older students!

3   Adults in the program say the tutors are great role models. The student tutors say they get a great <u>experience</u> from working with kids. It gives them confidence and improves their communication skills. It also gives them something fun and worthwhile to do after school.

Youth Coaches in Jacksonville

4   What's better than a play day at school? A play day with teen coaches! Just ask the six hundred students at a Florida elementary school. Each year, they spend a special day with dozens of high school athletes.

5   The teens teach all kinds of athletic skills. Some kids learn to slam-dunk a basketball while others learn the <u>fundamentals</u> of tennis. The teen coaches also give pointers on passing a football, swinging a bat, and dribbling a soccer ball. Even more importantly, the athletes take time to explain how they balance sports and schoolwork. Chances are good their message gets through, too. Their star-struck young listeners hang on every word the teens say!

Salsa Teachers in Boston

6   When asked what they wished their children could do after school, parents in one Boston community said, "Dance!" They probably wouldn't have <u>predicted</u> what happened next. Six older kids volunteered to learn Latin dance from professionals and become dance teachers!

7   The teens formed a group called *Ritmo en Acción* and began sharing the dance steps they learned. They taught classes at two elementary schools and one dance studio. The program grew quickly. More kids became teachers and more young children learned to dance. For many of the children, it was a way to learn more about Latin <u>culture</u>. For all the students, it was a chance to spend time with teen role models they admired.

8   Today, the program is a big success. Over three hundred children sign up and <u>participate</u> in the classes every year. Their instructors teach them salsa and other cultural dances—all free of charge! Both the instructors and their young students agree that dancing is a great way to have fun while staying out of trouble.

WANTED: Rock Stars and Role Models!

9 Do you like music and being in the spotlight? Would you like to have fun and make a difference in your community? Then join the coolest, hippest, happiest kids in town—River City Rock Stars!

10 The River City Rock Stars are student performers who dance and sing to their favorite music. The group meets at the River City Community Center one evening a week. Each meeting starts with pizza and a demonstration by Troy Robbins, a.k.a. Hard Rock Robbins. This local legend <u>originated</u> the group and is now its sponsor. He coaches Rock Star members in all aspects of performance. Each fall, Robbins creates a music video featuring that year's River City Rock Stars.

11 The best part of being a Rock Star is teaching young fans how to sing, dance, and have fun just like a Rock Star. Instead of being bored after school ends in the afternoon, Rock Stars teach songs and dance routines to struggling students in after-school workshops. The young students then take part in a Rock Star performance at their school.

12 Past Rock Star groups have done a <u>phenomenal</u> job of inspiring their young students. These letters from Rock Star fans say it all:

Dear Rock Stars,

13 *It was awesome learning to sing and dance with you. You told me that I have to keep up my grades to stay in the group. I wasn't making good grades then. Now I am doing better in school because I want to join the Rock Stars someday. Thank you, Rock Stars!*

Sincerely,
Gabriela

Dear Rock Stars,

14 *You really do rock! I was very shy, but after working with you I found out that I love to dance. Performing on stage was <u>incredible</u>! It helped me make new friends. Now I'm teaching my friends all those cool moves.*

Rock on,
Jesse

15 Would you like to help and inspire young students, too? Join us and take on a new and exciting role. Be someone young fans can admire. Be a Rock Star!

Rock Star Registration

Who: Sixth to eighth graders

16 **Requirements:** Good grades, teacher recommendations, parental permission

Where: River City Community Center

When: 7:00 P.M., Wednesday

GO ON ➡

1 According to the article, working in the Seattle after-school program made student tutors more—

A confident

B energetic

C interesting

D relaxed

2 Which generalization is supported by information in the section of the article called "Youth Coaches in Jacksonville"?

F Young children learn best by sitting quietly and listening.

G Young children have difficulty settling down after playing.

H Young children talk more when they have a big audience.

J Young children listen best to speakers whom they admire.

3 What does the word fundamentals mean in paragraph 5?

A Equipment

B Basics

C Stories

D Tricks

4 In paragraph 5, the phrase "hang on every word" means—

F watch the speaker's lips

G listen with close attention

H get confused by unfamiliar words

J question everything that is said

5 In paragraph 6, the word predicted means—

A said what would happen in the future

B doubted what could happen in the future

C waited for what would happen in the future

D demanded what should happen in the future

6 What words in paragraph 8 help the reader understand what participate means?

F *sign up*

G *free of charge*

H *instructors*

J *out of trouble*

7 What does the word originated mean in paragraph 10?

A Watched

B Funded

C Joined

D Started

8 Which word in paragraph 11 has a negative connotation?

F *fans*

G *sing*

H *bored*

J *routines*

GO ON

9 Which phrase is used to convince kids that joining the Rock Stars would be a good thing to do?

A *coolest, hippest, happiest kids in town*

B *dance and sing to their favorite music*

C *all aspects of performance*

D *"I found out that I love to dance."*

10 What does the word <u>phenomenal</u> mean in paragraph 12?

F Difficult

G Entertaining

H Remarkable

J Thoughtful

11 What is the author's reason for including the student letters in paragraphs 13 and 14?

A To show that most young kids have musical talent

B To demonstrate that written thoughts and feelings are powerful

C To prove that the River City Rock Stars can make a difference

D To convince people to be kind to kids who are shy

12 One similarity between the article and the flyer is that both suggest that volunteering helps kids—

F make new friends

G avoid wasting time

H become better athletes

J build career experience

13 One difference between the article and the flyer is that—

A the article is a work of fiction and the flyer is a work of nonfiction

B the article was written to inform and the flyer was written to persuade

C the article shows kids in a positive light and the flyer focuses on kids' faults

D the article is mainly about Latin music and the flyer is mainly about rock-and-roll

14 Which is a generalization supported by statements in both the article and the flyer?

F Younger children would rather dance than play sports.

G Younger children are motivated by attention from older children.

H Younger children get frustrated when they try to imitate older children.

J Younger children will not try unless someone older helps them.

15 Which word has the same suffix as the word <u>incredible</u>?

A reliable

B credit

C dribble

D sensible

GO ON

16 Which syllable in the word <u>experience</u> has the schwa sound?

F ex

G pe

H ri

J ence

17 What is the final syllable of the word <u>culture</u>?

A re

B ure

C ture

D ulture

GO ON

Read this selection. Then answer the questions that follow it.
Mark your answers on the Answer Document.

Winners

1   A crowd of students stood talking and laughing in the school courtyard while they waited for the morning bell to ring. Suddenly a whistle pierced the quiet morning. When Gary looked toward the sound, he saw Laney in her morning patrol vest blocking the entrance and <u>defying</u> Javier to take another step. Javier was a new student from Mexico who had been enrolled in Gary's class the day before.

2   "Where do you think you're going?" she demanded.

3   Javier glanced around sheepishly, embarrassed to be the focus of everyone's attention. Gary immediately realized that Javier didn't understand what was <u>happening</u> and stepped forward before the situation could <u>worsen</u>.

4   "Javier is a new student," he told Laney. He gestured for Javier to come stand with him. Javier gratefully hurried away from the door and Laney's suspicious glare.

5   "I don't understand," Javier said with a bewildered look.

6   Gary explained that they had to wait for the bell before going into the building, but Javier still seemed confused.

7   Just then the bell rang and Gary pointed toward the door. "Now, we can go into the classroom," he said.

8   Javier observed the students moving toward the door and then grinned and nodded enthusiastically. "We can go in!" he said pointing to the door.

9   As the rest of the students sat down and got out their materials for language arts, Mr. Parks explained to Javier that he should take his books and go to room 307 for his English lesson.

GO ON

10   When Gary saw the confused expression on Javier's face, he wrote down the room number on a scrap of paper. Gary pointed at Javier and then at the door. "You need to go to room 307," he said, handing Javier the paper.

11   Javier stared at the number then broke into a big smile. "I go here," he confirmed. "Thank you!"

12   Gary got a big kick out of the look that lit up Javier's face each time he figured out what someone meant. It was the same expression game show contestants get after giving the correct answer and winning a million dollars.

13   When it was time for geometry, Gary slumped in his chair and experienced his usual wave of dread. He was a competent student and did well in most subjects, but geometry was like a foreign language to him. Mathematics of any kind always made him feel like one big failure.

14   Just as Mr. Parks wrote a page number on the board, Javier returned and eagerly got out his geometry book. Gary watched as Javier slowly turned the pages and studied the diagrams. He looked as engrossed as Gary did when he pored over the latest skateboard catalog!

15   Mr. Parks drew a right triangle on the board, labeled two sides with measurements, and wrote an x next to the third side. Then he turned to face the class. Before he could begin to explain the concept of using the two given measurements to find the missing one, Javier's hand shot up into the air.

16   Mr. Parks looked pleased. "Would you like to demonstrate how to find the value of x?" he asked, extending the chalk to Javier.

17   Javier hurried to the board, quickly wrote the equation for finding x, and then solved it. Gary stared dumbfounded at Javier's neat, confident calculations.

18   "Excellent work, Javier!" exclaimed Mr. Parks, clearly delighted and surprised. "If you keep improving your English, you may soon be up here doing *my* job!"

GO ON

19   Javier returned to his seat, obviously happy to have shown his classmates that he was good at something, even if he didn't understand English well.

20   Gary leaned across the aisle and held up his open hand. Javier contemplated it for a minute and then seemed to recognize the gesture. As he gave Gary a high-five, he flashed his million-dollar winner's smile again.

21   Gary pointed to the geometry book in front of Javier and grimaced to show his exasperation. He shook his head and said, "*I* do not understand."

22   Javier grinned and jerked his thumb to his chest. "I understand. I can help!"

23   Javier did help. He and Gary met during lunch to study. Each time Gary took a wrong turn in his calculations, Javier found ways to get him back on track. He drew pictures, made gestures, and pointed, and somehow Gary made sense of it all. After they got through a lesson, Javier held up his hand for another high-five. "Hit my head," he said.

24   "You mean *hand*," Gary said laughing. "Javier, my friend, you definitely need some help with your English!"

25   Javier laughed, too. "You can help?"

26   Gary considered the idea and said, "I'll be your English tutor if you keep those geometry lessons coming."

27   Javier happily agreed and each afternoon he helped Gary with his geometry homework. Gary, in turn, helped Javier with English.

28   When Mr. Parks returned the week's homework on Friday afternoon, Gary was hesitant to look at his grades. What if he'd misunderstood Javier's lessons? <u>Reluctantly</u>, he looked at his homework pages to see how he'd done.

29   "Wow, Javier! These are the highest math grades I've gotten in years!" he said. Then he quickly added, "Thanks to your help, of course."

GO ON

30 "Yes, my friend," Javier said, nodding and holding up his hand for a high-five. "Hit my head!"

31 Javier grinned at his own joke, and then both boys burst out laughing.

32 "How about a skateboard lesson to thank you for tutoring me?" suggested Gary, "I'll teach you the English words for all the moves, too."

33 As the two headed to Gary's house to get skateboards, they were each wearing a million-dollar winner's smile.

18 Laney confronted Javier because he—

F wouldn't speak English to her

G tried to be the center of attention

H blew a whistle in the school courtyard

J tried to enter the class before the bell

19 What does the word <u>defying</u> mean in paragraph 1?

A Challenging

B Helping

C Inviting

D Questioning

GO ON

20 What does the phrase "got a big kick out of" mean in paragraph 12?

   F Was amused by

   G Was confused by

   H Was fascinated by

   J Was embarrassed by

21 What made Javier smile his "million-dollar winner's" smile?

   A Understanding English

   B Leaving the classroom

   C Studying his geometry book

   D Being the center of attention

22 Which word from the story has a negative connotation?

   F *demanded*

   G *explained*

   H *asked*

   J *suggested*

23 Which word is a synonym for <u>slumped</u> in paragraph 13?

   A Collapsed

   B Slouched

   C Stretched

   D Turned

24 What words help the reader understand the meaning of the word <u>competent</u> in paragraph 13?

   F *usual wave*

   G *did well*

   H *most subjects*

   J *big failure*

25 In this story, Gary compares—

   A geometry to a wave

   B skateboards to triangles

   C math to a foreign language

   D calculations to a wrong turn

26 Why is paragraph 13 important to this story?

   F It introduces the main characters.

   G It describes a change of story setting.

   H It introduces a new problem into the plot.

   J It explains the solution to the story problem.

27 What does the word <u>concept</u> mean in paragraph 15?

   A Idea

   B Mystery

   C Problem

   D Secret

28 Look at the action map and then answer the question that follows.

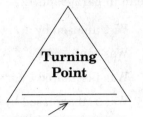

Event No. 2 Javier can't understand Mr. Parks' instructions.

Event No. 1 Javier is embarrassed in the courtyard.

Problem Javier feels out of place in his new school.

Which of these would go in the triangle labeled "Turning Point"?

F Javier studies his geometry book.

G Javier shows he is good at math.

H Javier leaves for an English lesson.

J Javier understands why the bell rang.

29 What happened right before Javier asked Gary for help learning English?

A Javier said *head* when he meant *hand*.

B Javier had to use gestures to tutor Gary.

C Javier told a joke that caused Gary to laugh.

D Javier had trouble understanding Mr. Parks's directions.

30 What does the word <u>reluctantly</u> mean in paragraph 28?

F Angrily

G Carefully

H Sadly

J Unwillingly

31 The reader can conclude that friendship with Gary will—

A lead Javier to neglect his studies

B cause Javier to become a morning patroller

C help Javier fit into American culture

D make Javier miss his friends in Mexico

32 Which word has the same sounds as the underlined letters in delig<u>ht</u>ed?

F assign

G digit

H signature

J weight

GO ON

33 Which syllable in the word <u>happening</u> is often pronounced with the schwa sound?

A hap

B pen

C ni

D ing

34 What is the final syllable of the word <u>worsen</u>?

F rsen

G orsen

H en

J sen

35 What is the base word of the word <u>figured</u>?

A fig

B figur

C figure

D gure

BE SURE TO MARK YOUR ANSWERS ON THE ANSWER DOCUMENT.

Writing: Revising and Editing

Read the introduction and the passage that follows it. Then read each question. Mark your answers on the Answer Document.

DeShaun wrote this description about his favorite summer place. He wants you to help him correct it. As you read DeShaun's description, think about the changes he should make to correct and improve it. Then answer the questions that follow.

My Favorite Summer Place

(1) When the sweltering days of summer arrive, I love to go to Crystal Falls because everything about that place makes me feel happy, cool, and refreshed.

(2) The adventure begins at the trailhead which is located in Roosevelt Community Park. (3) From there, my family hike the two-mile long path that crisscrosses the pine-covered mountainside and climbs toward the falls. (4) The steep, rocky trail is definitely not for casual hikers! (5) We know we have reached the final stretch of the journey. (6) We hear the falls roaring and splashing. (7) The moment we hear the thunder of the falls, my sister Dorie and I are tempted to rush ahead. (8) Niether of us can wait to plunge into the icy water! (9) My mother warns my sister not to hurry and she warns me, too. (10) The rocks on the trail

can be treacherous. (11) We continue to hike with our parents, but the anticipation is hard to contain!

(12) Finally, we reach the place where the giant waterfall pours over a tall, rocky cliff. (13) The cool mist from the waterfall feels delightful, so I pull off my shoes and eagerly wade into the shallow pool. (14) After cooling off, I walk around to the pool ledge behind the curtain of falling water. (15) Dorie looks blurry as she waves to me from the other side.

(16) I shout loudly to her. (17) She can't hear my words. (18) The roar of the falls is deafening.

(19) I hope you have the opportunity to visit Crystal Falls sometime. (20) It's a demanding hike up to the falls. (21) I guarantee you that it's worth the effort. (22) Once you experience it for yourself, I'm certain you'll agree that Crystal Falls is a summer paradise!

1 Which sentence could BEST be added before sentence 2?

A Swimming at the falls is a real treat.

B Crystal Falls is a tall, noisy waterfall.

C My sister Dorie can't hike as fast as I can.

D The hike to Crystal Falls is part of the fun.

2 What change should be made in sentence 3?

F Change *there* to **their**

G Change *hike* to **hikes**

H Change *climbs* to **climb**

J Change the period to a question mark

3 What is the BEST way to combine sentences 5 and 6?

A We know we have reached the final stretch of the journey but we hear the falls roaring and splashing.

B We know we have reached the final stretch of the journey when we hear the falls roaring and splashing.

C We know we have reached the final stretch of the journey unless we hear the falls roaring and splashing.

D We know we have reached the final stretch of the journey although we hear the falls roaring and splashing.

4 What change, if any, should be made in sentence 8?

F Change *Niether* to **Neither**

G Change *us* to **we**

H Change *plunge* to **plunged**

J Make no change

5 What is the BEST way to combine sentences 9 and 10?

A My mother warns me to not hurry and my sister, too, since the rocks can be treacherous.

B My mother warns my sister and I not to hurry, but the rocks on the trail can be treacherous.

C My mother warns my sister and I not to hurry and the rocks on the trail can be treacherous, too.

D My mother warns my sister and me not to hurry because the rocks on the trail can be treacherous.

6 What is the BEST way to combine sentences 16, 17, and 18?

F After I shout loudly to her, she can't hear my words so the roar of the falls is deafening.

G I shout loudly to her, and she can't hear my words but the roar of the falls is deafening.

H Since I shout loudly to her, she can't hear my words so the roar of the falls is deafening.

J Although I shout loudly to her, she can't hear my words because the roar of the falls is deafening.

7 What is the BEST way to combine sentences 20 and 21?

A It's a demanding hike up to the falls, I guarantee you that it's worth the effort.

B It's a demanding hike up to the falls, or I guarantee you that it's worth the effort.

C It's a demanding hike up to the falls, but I guarantee you that it's worth the effort.

D It's a demanding hike up to the falls and I guarantee you that it's worth the effort.

GO ON

Read the introduction and the passage that follows it. Then read each question. Mark your answers on the Answer Document.

Eva wrote this narrative about a canoe trip with her family. She would like you to read her story and suggest corrections and improvements she should make. When you finish reading, answer the questions that follow.

Our Crazy Canoe Trip

(1) Last summer my family went on a memorable canoe trip. (2) We expected a relaxed float down the river. (3) It turned out to be a wild ride!

(4) Dad and I paddled one canoe, and Mom paddled another with my little brother, Charlie. (5) Things started out nice and easy. (6) It wasn't long before things changed.

(7) In one narrow part of the river, trees extended out over the water. (8) As Charlie battled anacondas that he imagined were hanging from the branches, he made one serious errur. (9) He swatted at them with his paddle.

(10) Suddenly, we heard a deafening buzz, and we realized that Charlie had disturbed a beehive! (11) Mom yelled, "Everyone into the water!"

(12) Minutes later, the bees had departed but we were in a mess.

(13) Both canoes were overturned and our supplies floating around us.

(14) Thankfully, our life jackets kept us afloat while we loaded the canoes and started down the river again.

(15) Our next mishap occurred at the rapids. (16) I love zipping over rushing water, but this time the water was *too* fast. (17) It spun our canoe sideways and shoved us up onto a large rock. (18) Swirling below us, our paddles couldn't even reach the water! (19) Thinking quickly, Dad got out and pushed the canoe free. (20) He barely made it back into our canoe before it rushed downstream!

(21) Back in calm water, Charlie dipped his sunglasses in the river to rinse them. (22) The sparkle of the metal frames attracted some fish and one jumped into the air. (23) Plop! (24) It landed right in Charlie's lap. (25) The fish gave such a start that Charlie jumped up, causing the boat to tip. (26) Charlie, Mom, and the fish all ended up in the river.

(27) We repacked their canoe we all agreed that our next trip would be a bike ride!

8 What is the BEST way to combine sentences 2 and 3?

F So we expected a relaxed float down the river it turned out to be a wild ride!

G We expected a relaxed float down the river since it turned out to be a wild ride!

H Although we expected a relaxed float down the river, it turned out to be a wild ride!

J We expected a relaxed float down the river, or it turned out to be a wild ride!

9 What is the BEST way to combine sentences 5 and 6?

A Things started out nice and easy, it wasn't long before things changed.

B Things started out nice and easy, or it wasn't long before things changed.

C Things started out nice and easy, but it wasn't long before things changed.

D Since things started out nice and easy, it wasn't long before things changed.

10 What change should be made in sentence 8?

F Insert a comma after *Charlie*

G Change *battled* to **battles**

H Change *errur* to **error**

J Delete the comma after *branches*

11 What change should be made in sentence 13?

A Change *canoes* to **canoe**

B Change *and* to **but**

C Insert **were** before *floating*

D Change *us* to **we**

12 What is the BEST way to revise sentence 18?

F Swirling, our paddles couldn't even reach below the water!

G Our paddles couldn't even reach the water swirling below us!

H Swirling below our paddles, we couldn't even reach the water!

J Our paddles, swirling below us, couldn't even reach the water!

13 What change should be made in sentence 25?

A Insert **him** after *gave*

B Insert a comma after *start*

C Change *jumped* to **jumps**

D Change *the boat* to **it**

14 What is the BEST way to revise sentence 27?

F We repacked their canoe, we all agreed that our next trip would be a bike ride!

G As we repacked their canoe, we all agreed that our next trip would be a bike ride!

H We repacked their canoe, or we all agreed that our next trip would be a bike ride!

J Until we repacked their canoe, we all agreed that our next trip would be a bike ride!

GO ON

> **Read the introduction and the passage that follows it. Then read each question. Mark your answers on the Answer Document.**

Molly is writing a research report on water pollution. She would like you to read her first draft and suggest ways she can revise and improve it. When you finish reading, answer the questions that follow.

Water Pollution

(1) However, it is still a big problem. (2) That is why it be important for everyone to try and do their part to help. (3) Doing everyday things the right way can help prevent water pollution.

(4) Each weekend, many people spend working in their yards. (5) Some people might use chemicals to kill weeds and pests. (6) They might also spread fertilizer to help plants and flowers grow. (7) These chemicals can soak into the ground and pollute underground water sources. (8) It is

important to read the labels, to help limit the impact of these things on

the water supply, on these products. (9) The chemicals should be used in

moderation and only as directed. (10) People can also seek out natural

alternatives to chemicals for pest control or fertilizer.

(11) People can also cause water pollution if they wash their cars or

changes the oil in their cars. (14) Soap and oily dirt from car washing can

flow into the street and then into storm drains. (15) It is important to only

use soaps that are not harmful to the environment when washing a car.

(16) Taking their cars to a mechanic for an oil change. (17) Instead of some

people change the oil themselves. (18) When doing this, it is important that

the old oil is taken to a place that accepts old oil for proper disposal.

(19) It is expensive to make polluted water useble again.

(20) Preventing pollution in the first place makes good sense. (21) People

can make a difference if they follow a few simple rules.

15 Which sentence could BEST be added before sentence 1?

   A Some towns depend on water for fishing or recreation.

   B Many laws have been passed to prevent water pollution.

   C Cars can cause water pollution in several different ways.

   D All humans need water to survive, especially when it is hot outside.

16 What change should be made in sentence 2?

   F Change *be* to **is**

   G Change *try* to **tried**

   H Change *and* to **or**

   J Insert a comma after *part*

17 What change should be made in sentence 4?

   A Delete the comma after *weekend*

   B Change *many* to *lots and lots of*

   C Insert **time** after *spend*

   D Change *their* to *there*

18 What is the BEST way to revise sentence 8?

   F It is important to read, to help limit the impact of these things on the water supply, the labels on these products.

   G To help limit the impact of these things on the water supply, it is important to read the labels on these products.

   H On the water supply, it is important to read the labels on these products, to help limit the impact of these things.

   J To help limit the impact of these things on these products, it is important to read the labels on the water supply.

19 What change, if any, should be made in sentence 11?

   A Change *cause* to **causes**

   B Change *if* to **although**

   C Change *changes* to **change**

   D Make no change

20 What is the BEST way to combine sentences 16 and 17?

   F Instead of taking their cars to a mechanic for an oil change, because some people change the oil themselves.

   G Taking their cars to a mechanic for an oil change, instead of some people change the oil themselves.

   H Instead of taking their cars to a mechanic for an oil change, some people change the oil themselves.

   J Taking their cars to a mechanic for an oil change, so some people change the oil themselves instead of.

21 What change should be made in sentence 19?

   A Change *is* to **are**

   B Change *make* to **made**

   C Delete *water* after **polluted**

   D Change *useble* to **usable**

BE SURE TO MARK YOUR ANSWERS ON THE ANSWER DOCUMENT.

Name _____ Date _____

Writing: Written Composition

Read the story below and respond to the prompt that follows it.

Education in Japan

Can you imagine attending school on Saturdays instead of having time off to relax? Many Japanese families pay so that students can do just that! Succeeding in school is extremely important in Japanese culture. That is why parents pay for their children to attend extra classes called *juku* in the evenings and on weekends.

Like American students, Japanese students attend elementary school for six years and junior high school for three years. Those nine years of education are mandatory for all students. However, the three years of high school are optional. Students must pass a difficult test and pay tuition if they want to go beyond junior high school. In spite of these obstacles, most students meet the high standards and pay the fees so they can graduate from high school. Very few ever drop out.

At the beginning of the school day, Japanese students perform a morning ritual of bowing and giving their teacher a respectful greeting. Many wear school uniforms, which they are expected to keep neat and clean at all times.

The school curriculum in Japan is challenging and generally includes memorizing a great deal of information. Elementary and junior high school students usually work as a class rather than individually or in small groups as American students often do. The Japanese students sometimes recite their lessons aloud and in unison. The classroom teacher may also teach students to play musical instruments.

At lunch, the students usually go to the cafeteria and prepare their own food. While in the kitchen, they wear masks to avoid contaminating food and spreading germs. They return to their classroom to eat and then clean up after the meal. As in America, recess is spent playing active games, such as soccer.

Once afternoon classes are over, students in most schools are expected to clean their classroom and school. They scrub, sweep, and mop until everything is sparkling clean. Then, as they leave their classroom, they bow to their teachers and thank them.

After dismissal from class, most students remain at school for several more hours to attend clubs or extra classes. They learn computer skills, English, sports, card games, homemaking skills, and music. Many students also attend *juku* for tutoring to help them keep up with their most difficult subjects of study. Others go to *juku* courses that prepare them for the challenging high school entrance exams.

The diligent work that Japanese students do clearly shows in test score results. In exams that compare student achievement in countries around the world, Japanese students always rank at or near the top.

> Do you think American schools should be more like Japanese schools?
> Use details from the passage and your own school experiences to
> explain why or why not. Write an opinion essay explaining your ideas.

Use a separate sheet of paper to plan your composition. Then write your composition
on the lined pages that follow.

The information in the box below will help you remember what you should think about
when you write your composition.

REMEMBER—YOU SHOULD

❑ write whether American schools should
be more like Japanese schools

❑ identify the topic and state your
opinion in the introduction

❑ give reasons and list details from the
text to support your opinion

❑ present information in logical order

❑ summarize your opinion in the
conclusion

❑ try to use correct spelling,
capitalization, punctuation, grammar,
and complete sentences

Name _____ Date _____

_____

_____

_____

_____

_____

_____

_____

_____

_____

_____

_____

_____

_____

_____

_____

_____

_____

Name _____ Date _____

_____

_____

_____

_____

_____

_____

_____

_____

_____

_____

_____

_____

_____

_____

Reading

Read this selection. Then answer the questions that follow it.
Mark your answers on the Answer Document.

Not What I Thought

1 Even as a little child, Emma hated spaghetti because she thought
it was slimy. She couldn't handle tapioca pudding or cottage cheese
either. When Emma heard that her class was going to make pasta
from scratch, she groaned piteously.

2 "Pasta is disgusting—it reminds me of worms," Emma complained
secretly to Jonah. They both chuckled, stopping only when Mrs.
Buckingham glanced sternly in their direction.

3 Friday morning, the entire class gathered in the cafeteria kitchen
and split into work groups. Each group was to make tomato sauce,
pasta, or antipasto salad. Just as Emma had feared, she was assigned
to the "pasta" group, along with her friends Jonah and Arturo.

4 After the three washed their hands, Jonah measured three pounds
of flour and poured it into a bowl. Arturo carved a crater in the hill of
flour, and then Jonah cracked a dozen eggs into it. Meanwhile, Emma
stood by herself with her arms crossed, wishing her stomach would
stop somersaulting at the sight of all those slimy eggs. Since Mrs.
Buckingham had given each of the groups a detailed set of instructions,
everyone knew exactly what to do. The next step would be to mix the
dough by hand.

5   "Each group has to be certain that everyone participates," Mrs. Buckingham called out to the entire class, and of course, Arturo and Jonah stared directly at Emma.

6   "This step is all yours," Jonah announced unsympathetically with a mischievous grimace.

7   "You'd really rather do the kneading, wouldn't you?" Emma pleaded, looking sideways at Arturo.

8   "Nope, not me," Arturo replied, grinning and obviously hoping for a little extra drama.

9   Giving up hope, Emma grimaced as she pushed up her right sleeve and gripped the mixing bowl. She closed her eyes as she inserted her free hand directly into the eggs. Making a face at the sloshing sound they made as she turned the bowl, she squished them into the flour with her fingers. She did it again, faster and faster, and suddenly she realized that she enjoyed the rhythm and the feel of the dough. It was soft like skin, yet sticky like gum. As she continued to spin the bowl and mix them, the flour and eggs became one perfect pillow of dough.

10   Mrs. Buckingham smiled approvingly at Emma. "Remember, Emma, as soon as the dough is an even consistency, knead it for twelve more minutes. Those twelve minutes are the secret to good pasta."

11   "Give us a turn, too," Arturo and Jonah teased, but they could tell she wasn't going to give up her share of the group's work. After twelve minutes, Jonah covered the dough with a towel, and the three of them cleaned up their work table. After the dough had risen, Mrs. Buckingham set up the pasta making machine. Arturo and Jonah took turns putting dough into the top of the machine and rotating the handle, while Emma caught the strands of fresh linguini in a clean bowl.

12   By 11:00 A.M., the class meal was almost ready: sauce simmered on the stove, bread toasted in the oven, and antipasto platters waited in the refrigerators. At 11:30 A.M., a huge pot of water started boiling to cook the pasta, and three minutes later, Emma's group drained the linguini and put it into big bowls, enough for everyone.

GO ON

Name _____ Date _____

13   "Well, what do you think?" Mrs. Buckingham asked Emma, who was slurping a noodle into her mouth.

14   Emma answered her teacher with a big "thumbs up." After she finished chewing and wiping some of the sauce from her chin, she admitted, "It's absolutely delicious—not what I thought at all."

---

1   Which of the following events takes place first on the day of the project?

A Mrs. Buckingham smiles at Emma.

B Jonah measures flour into a bowl.

C The students wash their hands.

D Arturo hopes for a little drama.

2   Which is an important theme in this story?

F Teamwork

G Family

H Compassion

J Honesty

3   What quality does Emma possess that is important to the story's plot?

A She is curious about anything new.

B She has a big appetite.

C She is disgusted by slimy things.

D She gets along well with classmates.

4   The children are preparing the spaghetti lunch for—

F all of their classmates

G everyone in the school

H their teachers and parents

J the principal and teachers

5   Which sentence best shows the connection between the setting and the plot of the story?

A While making spaghetti with Arturo and Jonah, Emma faces her fear and learns something new.

B Emma, Arturo, and Jonah are students, and Mrs. Buckingham is one of their teachers.

C Emma, Arturo, and Jonah contribute to a meal that includes spaghetti and antipasto salad.

D Required to take part in a group activity at school, Emma faces her fear and learns something new.

6   Which of these statements is most likely true of this story?

F Something like this probably happened to the author.

G The story could be based on a real experience.

H The character Emma is a stand-in for the story's author.

J Nothing like this ever happened in real life.

GO ON

Name _____ Date _____

Winter's End
by Pamela Love

Late February
Icicles drip days away
Splashing into spring

Do You Want to Write a Poem?

by Myra Cohn Livingston
illustarted by Julie Kim

1   The word "haiku" means "a beginning phrase." A haiku was originally the beginning of a longer poem; the first 17 syllables were written to introduce the reader to the rest of the poem. Today haiku is considered a poetic form in itself.

2   Some of you might know that the short poem at the top of this page is called a *haiku*. Haiku poetry has been written in Japan for hundreds of years and has become popular in the United States. There

GO ON

are specific rules for writing haiku, but all most people know is that the poem is made up of 17 syllables, that it is usually written in three lines, and that it does not use rhyme.

3   The first rule for writing a haiku is that the poem must always refer to something in nature or use what is called a "season word." Many of the haiku you read refer to nature symbols of Japan, but unless you have visited Japan, you will be better off writing about things you know in your own country. For instance, if you read about a cherry blossom in a Japanese haiku, it means spring. Different flowers are more familiar signs of spring in other places, so you might want to write about snowdrops, crocuses, or daffodils if they grow near you. You do not have to use the words "spring," "summer," "autumn," or "winter" to name the season when you write a haiku—the word "snow," for example, becomes a season word for "winter."

4   Another rule is that the haiku must be about *one* thing only. A haiku is not a poem that describes several different subjects or events. A good writer of haiku looks at one thing carefully and writes about only that.

5   The third rule is that a haiku must be written as though you are just seeing or experiencing what you write about. It should happen *now*, not yesterday or the day before or last year. Therefore, haiku is usually written in the present tense.

6   The next rule is that a good haiku must present a clear picture of something you want to think about further. It paints a picture in words that stirs your imagination and makes you eager to find out more.

7   Remember, too, that when you have only 17 syllables, it is important to choose your words carefully and not repeat any.

8   A good way to get haiku ideas is to look outside or take a walk. Maybe you'll see a snail as the poet Issa did:

Well! Hello down there friend snail!
When did you arrive in such a hurry?

GO ON

9   Or you might want to warn the butterflies, as the poet Shosen did:

Butterflies, beware!
Needles of pines can be sharp
in a gusty wind!

10   If you are just beginning to write haiku, you might find it easier to write as though you were talking to whatever subject you choose—a butterfly, cricket, fly, or snail; or even the moon, stars, sun, wind, or rain.

11   Now it's your turn to write a haiku! Choose your words carefully, draw a vivid picture with them, and let your imagination run wild …

7 According to the article, the first step in writing a haiku is to—

A repeat key words

B use past tense

C count syllables

D observe nature

8 Which statement is true of a haiku?

F It must rhyme.

G It describes several subjects.

H It uses season words.

J It is in Japanese.

9 The poem, "Winter's End," compares the—

A coming of spring and melting icicles

B end of fall and growing icicles

C coming of winter and soft rain

D end of spring and violent storms

10 Which kind of literary device is used in the haiku about snails?

F Simile: Snails are compared to fast cars.

G Irony: Snails are not able to hurry.

H Personification: Snails are given human traits.

J Symbol: Snails represent an abstract idea.

11 The writer of the article suggests that—

A anyone can write a haiku

B only Japanese writers can write a haiku

C only skilled poets can write a haiku

D people should learn how to write a haiku in school

12 Which sentence is the best summary of paragraph 3?

F Haiku always contain the names of flowers.

G Haiku are set in specific seasons.

H Haiku are set in specific seasons in Japan.

J Haiku always contain the names of seasons.

GO ON

Name _____ Date _____

Alaska's Long, Cold Race

1   Alaska's Iditarod Trail Sled Dog Race, held once every year in March, is the longest dogsled race in the world. During the Iditarod, dog teams and their human leaders, called mushers, cover over 1,150 miles in ten to seventeen days.

History

2   Beginning in the 1880s, with the discovery of gold, prospectors flocked to Alaska to seek their fortune. Arriving on the coast, they followed trails to the interior, using dog-drawn sleds to travel hundreds of miles of frozen wilderness. Their main route from Anchorage to Nome is known today as the Iditarod Trail.

3   In the 1920s, airplanes began to replace dogsleds as a means of getting around the Alaskan wilderness. In the early 1960s, the snowmobile (the "iron dog") was invented, and dogsled teams fell into disuse. However, the one-hundredth anniversary of Alaska's statehood was approaching. Increased interest in Alaska's spirit and history led to the idea for a dogsled race.

4   A local historian named Dorothy Page, one of the planners for the 1967 centennial, had the idea. She suggested the Iditarod Trail as the route, and musher groups backed her enthusiastically. Volunteers, who have played a big part in the race from the beginning, began to clear brush from the long disused trail.

5   In 1967 the first Iditarod was run as part of Alaska's Centennial. That initial race was only 27 miles long. By 1973, the Trail had been restored all the way to Nome, and twenty-two mushers raced over its 1,150-mile length. The race has been held every year since then.

Route

6   The race begins in Anchorage (see map), and the teams wind through many towns, or checkpoints, such as Rainy Pass and Safety, before crossing the finish line in Nome. In even-numbered years, the race

68

follows a northern route. In odd-numbered years, it follows a southern route that includes the old mining town of Iditarod. This change of route allows time for smaller towns to recover from the impact of the race.

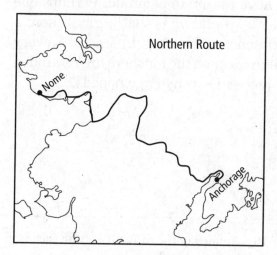
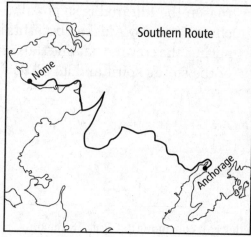

Competitors

7   According to the official Web site of the Iditarod, the competitors come from all walks of life and all over the world: "Fishermen, lawyers, doctors, miners, artists, natives, Canadians, Swiss, French, and others." About fifty to seventy mushers finish the grueling race each year.

8   Some of the mushers have made Iditarod history. For example, Rick Swenson is a five-time winner. He's also entered twenty Iditarod races and never finished out of the top ten. In 1978, Dick Mackey won the race from Swenson by only one second. Four-time winner Susan Butcher was the first woman to place in the top ten. Libby Riddles was the first woman to win the race, in 1985.

9   Of course the teams are really contending with nature. March in Alaska can be brutal. The trail runs through wild mountains and dense forests and across rivers whose winter ice may be melting. Temperatures can be far below freezing, especially at night. Blizzards, sleet, and biting wind add to the hazards.

Popularity

10   The Iditarod attracts competitors because it is the longest, most challenging race of its kind in the world. Only the best teams can vie for the prize and those that finish have reason to be proud. Perhaps one reason the Iditarod is so popular with spectators is that it gives them a chance to enjoy Alaska's breathtaking natural beauty. In any case, every spring, the crowds that line the trail to cheer on the mushers are reminded of the state's spirit and its history, just as Dorothy Page hoped.

---

13 The reader can conclude that Rick Swenson—

A hates to lose a race

B is a highly skilled musher

C is the oldest musher

D raced in the first Iditarod

14 Which statement about the Iditarod's location is true?

F The area where the race is run has a harsh climate.

G The race takes place during the winter.

H The Iditarod Trail was created for the race.

J The race takes place in Canada.

15 The facts in the section headed "History" are arranged in—

A order of importance

B random order

C chronological order

D order of difficulty

16 An idea of the difficulty of the race is given by facts about—

F mushers who run the race

G the land and the weather conditions

H the popularity of the race

J transportation in Alaska

17 Which event came first?

A Rick Swenson wins

B Discovery of gold in Alaska

C Alaska's Centennial

D Complete restoration of the Trail

GO ON

Name _____   Date _____

Read this selection. Then answer the questions that follow it.
Mark your answers on the Answer Document.

Beginner's Mind

1   Back in the spring, when she chose to go to Tae Kwon Do camp, Felicia was really excited about her summer. However, now that she's here, she feels differently. She's been interested in martial arts for many years but never practiced before. Many of the campers she has met since arriving here this morning have been coming to this camp for several years. She's sure she will be the only one with a beginner's belt. She looks at herself in the bathroom mirror, smooths her new white uniform, and wonders how she looks.

2   Nevertheless, Felicia joins a group of laughing girls on their way to the practice hall. They introduce themselves, retelling the joke that had amused them, and Felicia laughs with the group. At the entrance to the practice room, Jill, a third-year camper, introduces herself as Felicia's partner. Adjusting Felicia's uniform, she explains how partnering works: "You'll take the place immediately behind me, and follow what I do. I'm sure you'll do great."

3   Removing their shoes, the campers enter the big, bright space and silently line up in straight columns, each separated by a comfortable distance. The practice room seems calm and inviting, and even though the windows are shaded, the shapes of the mountains surrounding the camp are visible. The wooden floor feels solid under Felicia's feet as she lines up behind Jill, thankfully, in the very back row.

4   Annie, Felicia's counselor and today's instructor, steps to the front of the room, places her palms together in front of her chest, and bows from the waist. Everyone else returns the gesture.

5   "Welcome," says Annie. "We have a few beginners with us, so let's begin with the rules; we'll recite these at each session." Felicia is familiar with these, since they were printed on the materials she received with her uniform.

6   As she echoes them with the campers, she glances around secretly to see several other girls with beginner's belts in the back row. "I'm not the only beginner," she thinks, relieved.

7   "We will begin today with a stretching demonstration. Stretching is one of the most important parts of practice, and this series of stretches will begin each practice session." Annie demonstrates a series of stretches, and the campers do the stretches with her. Then the campers do the series by themselves while Annie walks around, correcting their positions as necessary. The stretches are complicated, so Felicia keeps her eyes glued on Jill. At one point she's almost touching the floor with one leg crook-kneed in front of her and the other leg stretched straight out behind, but she's concentrating too hard on doing the stretch correctly to worry about what she looks like.

8   The stretching continues, and Felicia starts to feel more comfortable. She likes the fact that all the campers are doing the same thing; she doesn't feel out of place, just part of the group.

9   After a while, Annie dismisses the class with a bow and Felicia is surprised to find it is lunchtime. She follows the campers as they silently exit the practice room. Outside, Jill approaches Felicia and says, "See, you're a natural. I told you you'd do great." Felicia smiles and thanks Jill for being her partner. No longer worried about the summer ahead, Felicia grins widely and can't wait until the afternoon practice session, in which Annie has promised to teach them some basic moves.

18 Most of this story takes place in—

   F   Felicia's home in the city

   G   a practice hall at a martial arts camp

   H   a sleeping cabin at a martial arts camp

   J   a dining hall at a Tae Kwon Do camp

19 Which of the following events happens last in the story?

   A   Jill gives Felicia a compliment.

   B   Felicia arrives at a summer camp.

   C   Annie welcomes the class to camp.

   D   Felicia looks at herself in a mirror.

20 Which is a theme of this story?

   F   A change of scene can make all the difference.

   G   Gentle encouragement promotes confidence.

   H   Hard exercise creates strong bodies.

   J   Martial arts are a means of self-defense.

21 This story is—

   A   a drama

   B   a novel

   C   science fiction

   D   a short story

22 What literary device does the author use to move the plot forward?

   F   Dialogue

   G   Foreshadowing

   H   Chapters

   J   Flashback

GO ON

> **Read this selection. Then answer the questions that follow it.**
> **Mark your answers on the Answer Document.**

Keeping Cool with Crickets

by Lois Jacobson
illustarted by Karen Ritz

1   "Konnichiwa. Good Afternoon," my Japanese neighbor called through the door. "I have brought a present to welcome you to Japan."

2   The package was very small and tied with delicately curled ribbons. What could such a tiny box contain? Puzzled, I lifted the lid, and there, nestled in whisper-thin tissue paper, was a blue-and-white dish. It was shaped like a miniature bottle cap, and its cracked, glazed surface made it look very old—and very special.

3   "It's a water dish for crickets." My new friend's voice almost chirped with delight.

4   "What does one do with a water dish for crickets?" I asked.

5   "You put it inside a cricket house."

6   "Cricket house?"

7   "If you are going to live in Tokyo during the heat of the summer," said my neighbor, "you must learn to keep cool with crickets!"

8   Now I was curious. I soon learned that in the Far East, people have kept crickets as pets for centuries. In the past they housed them in cages made of bamboo or delicately carved jade, which they hung from the eaves or porches of their weathered homes. Bamboo cages are still used today, but most children keep their crickets in plastic cages the colors of cool lime or raspberry sherbet.

9   During the hot, breathless summer months, Japanese parks are filled with laughing children and parents, armed with butterfly nets and small towels, pursuing their prey. The crickets are hard to catch because their hind legs are well developed for jumping. But once trapped in a net or under a small towel, they can be put in cages or small glass jars with air holes in the lids.

10   For people who can't catch their own, there are cricket vendors. I soon found myself at a market stall eyeing a plump, brownish black cricket. The vendor put my selection in a cardboard container. From the vibrations, I knew that my cricket didn't like being shut up inside. He needed a house.

11   He and I scouted out the local cricket real-estate market. Our search ended in a cluttered stall filled with bamboo wares. Tucked in a corner, amid baskets and flower containers, was a miniature Japanese house made of slender bamboo reeds. It was just right for the antique water dish—and, of course, for my cricket.

12   Using many hand gestures, the kimono-clad shopkeeper explained that the bottom of the house must be layered with just enough soil to anchor the filled water dish. Crickets, she added, love raw potatoes, cucumbers, bits of water-soaked bread, and leafy greens—all in cricket-size portions.

13   Charlie and I were eager to move in. I knew he was a Charlie because only male crickets chirp. Crickets have

four wings that lie flat, one pair over the other on top of their bodies. By raising the upper pair of wings and rubbing one wing over the other, the males produce their singing or chirping sound.

14   Each song has a meaning. Some serve as calling songs to attract females, others as courting songs. In Japan it is said that they sing, *"Kata sase suso sase samusa ga kuruzo,"* or "Sew your sleeves, sew your skirts, the cold weather is coming."

15   Charlie Cricket was quiet as I put down a thin layer of dirt in his home, stocked his pantry with lettuce and potatoes, and added the antique water dish. Now, how was I going to get that bundle of energy from carton to house? I lifted the cardboard flap, and Charlie eyed me, ready to do battle. Using all ten fingers, a soothing voice, and lots of encouragement, I soon had him safely in his house.

16   Tired from the summer heat, I hung Charlie from the eaves on the balcony. Nearby, wind chimes tinkled melodiously with each gentle breeze.

17   "Cool me off," I pleaded. "Chirp, Charlie, chirp." The heat hung suspended around me. And Charlie chirped! The garden bells tinkled in accompaniment. It was as if the enchanting sounds and the whirring of cricket wings awakened the air and stirred it about me ever so gently.

18   "Sing, Charlie!" His song sounded like the clinking of ice cubes in chilled crystal goblets. The heat seemed to waft away. I had learned the Japanese art of keeping cool with crickets.

23 The narrator of this story is—

   A a Japanese citizen

   B new to Japan

   C suspicious of customs

   D afraid of crickets

24 The narrator acquires a cricket by—

   F catching one in a net

   G receiving one as a gift

   H buying one in a market

   J finding one on the balcony

25 Which of the following is a theme of the story?

   A People can benefit from animals.

   B Only male crickets chirp.

   C People speak different languages.

   D Only crickets are kept in houses.

26 Which sentence from the story contains figurative language?

   F *Each song has a meaning.*

   G *The heat seemed to waft away.*

   H *His song sounded like the clinking of ice cubes in chilled crystal goblets.*

   J *The crickets are hard to catch because their hind legs are well developed for jumping.*

27 How does the dialogue of the story support the setting?

   A The narrator asks many questions.

   B The neighbor expresses concern for the narrator.

   C The narrator hears foreign words and phrases.

   D The neighbor speaks to the narrator through the door.

> **Read this selection. Then answer the questions that follow it.
> Mark your answers on the Answer Document.**

The American Bald Eagle: A Recovery Success Story

1   In 1782, the bald eagle—the only eagle native to North America—was adopted as the national bird and the symbol of the United States. Even so, in the one hundred and seventy years that followed, this marvelous bird was brought to near extinction. Wildlife experts believe that, in 1800, there were as many as 100,000 nesting eagles in America. By 1963, there were only 417 eagle pairs left in the lower forty-eight states. Today, due to recovery efforts, the number of eagle pairs exceeds 9,000. Why did the eagle population drop, and how did it bounce back so dramatically?

2   As the country grew and people moved further west, the eagles' world changed. People usually settled first along rivers and near lakes, disturbing the eagles' nesting places. People outnumbered eagles and took over the food supply. They saw eagles as a threat to their own animals and killed the birds on sight. Also, many eagles were killed in traps meant for wolves, or they died from lead poisoning after eating small animals killed with lead shot.

3   By 1940, the eagle population was dangerously low. People recognized that something had to be done or the bird would disappear altogether. In that year, Congress passed the Bald Eagle Protection Act, which made it illegal to kill eagles. Also, during the 1940s and 1950s, many dams and reservoirs were built to give energy and water supplies to people. This had the fortunate side effect of providing good eagle nesting sites, which allowed the eagle population to slowly grow.

4   Then, a new threat to eagles arrived: DDT, a chemical used to kill off mosquitoes and insects that attack crops. Rains washed DDT into rivers and lakes where it was absorbed by water plants and animals. Fish ate the poison-carrying plants and animals, and eagles ate those fish. DDT did not kill eagles directly; instead, it affected their ability to make strong shells for their eggs. Fewer and fewer eggs survived or hatched.

5   Congress recognized that there was a problem with the eagle population and listed the bald eagle as endangered on March 11, 1967. It soon became clear that the eagles had to be protected from DDT. It was banned in 1973. Congress then wrote the Endangered Species Act. This law lists animals and plants as either threatened or endangered. Listed as threatened means that they are in danger but not likely to disappear, while endangered animals and plants are likely to disappear. The act also gives the government the power to protect these animals and plants.

6   The U.S. Fish and Wildlife Service divided the country into five eagle recovery regions. Each region wrote its own recovery plan. It also set eagle population goals. Plans included programs in which bald eagles were hatched and then placed in the wild, protecting the places where bald eagles were seen nesting from development, and teaching people about the eagles. These programs were a success, and by 1995 the eagle population goals were met. The bald eagle was taken off the endangered list. While the bald eagle now flies over much of the United States, it will still be protected so that the population can continue to grow.

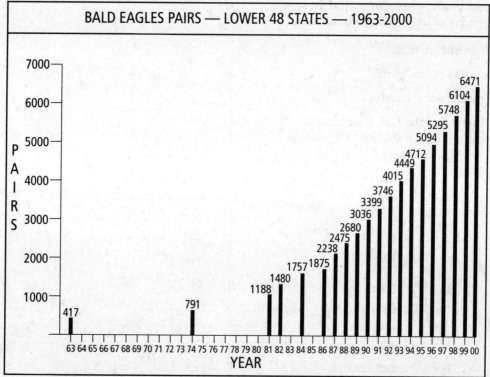

This chart shows the number of bald eagles from 1963 to 2000.

GO ON

Name _____ Date _____

28 The author's purpose in paragraph 4 is to—

F describe how DDT works

G explain how DDT affected eagles

H present statistics about DDT

J persuade readers not to use DDT

29 For which topic does this article offer the most support?

A Eagles like to nest near dams and reservoirs.

B All chemicals are dangerous to animals and birds.

C Environmental laws and action can work.

D The government is a threat to certain populations.

30 The most likely source for a student to see photographs of bald eagles would be—

F an online dictionary

G an atlas of the world

H a recent encyclopedia

J a history of the U.S. Congress

31 The most efficient way to find out what species are endangered would be to—

A do an online search for *endangered species*

B write to a member of Congress and ask

C check your local library for books about eagles

D find a book written by the author of this passage

32 What was a major cause of the decline in the bald eagle population?

F Changes in the levels of rivers and lakes

G Changes in temperature and rainfall

H Animal predators who hunted eagles

J Human population growth

BE SURE TO MARK YOUR ANSWERS ON THE ANSWER DOCUMENT.

Writing: Revising and Editing

After visiting the Grand Canyon, Mikaela wrote a report about it. She would like you to read it and think about the changes she needs to make. When you finish reading, answer the questions that follow.

A Canyon That's Grand

(1) Each year, almost five million people travel to Arizona to visit the Grand Canyon National Park, and there's a good reason for this popularity. (2) Because of its big big size and breathtaking beauty, the Grand Canyon is one of the seven natural wonders of the world. (3) The Great Barrier Reef is another natural wonder of the world.

(4) Over the ages, the rushing waters of the Colorado River have slowly cut through the sandstone and limestone rock, creating the 277-mile-long gorge known as the Grand Canyon. (5) The Colorado River separates the

two sides of the park into the North Rim and the South Rim. (6) Standing

on one side of the canyon. (7) You can see the river about one mile below.

(8) The canyon may be deep, but it is wide, too. (9) In some places, the

span between the two sides is about 15 miles!

(10) As part of their explorashon, many people want to hike from

one side of the canyon to the other. (11) In order to do so, they can walk

across a narrow bridge that is 70 feet above the River. (12) Hikers begin

the 21-mile trek at the top of the canyon (called the rim), climb down the

canyon, cross the bridge, and climb up the other side.

(13) If you visit the Grand Canyon, remember to bring a camera

to capture the spectacular scenes? (14) The scenery will appear to

transform before your eyes as the sun rises and sets. (15) The hue of the

canyon's rocky walls changes from brown to pink to orange. (16) Observe

the dramatic waterfalls and fascinating wildlife. (17) Photograph the

dramatic waterfalls and fascinating wildlife. (18) You will absolutely be

amazed, and so will the people who look at your photographs.

1 What change should be made in sentence 2?

   A Change *big big* to **massive**

   B Insert a comma after *size*

   C Delete the comma after *beauty*

   D Change *is* to *are*

2 What revision is needed in sentences 6 and 7?

   F Standing on one side of the canyon you can see the river about one mile below the canyon.

   G When you stand on one side of the canyon, and you can see the river about one mile below.

   H Standing on one side of the canyon, you can see the river about one mile below.

   J Standing about one mile below the canyon, you can see the river on one side.

3 What change should be made in sentence 10?

   A Change *explorashon* to **exploration**

   B Change *want* to **wanted**

   C Change *hike* to **hiked**

   D Change *canyon* to **Canyon**

4 What change should be made in sentence 11?

   F Delete the comma after *so*

   G Change *can walk* to **walks**

   H Change *feet* to **foot**

   J Change *River* to **river**

5 What change should be made in sentence 13?

   A Change the comma to a period

   B Change *bring* to **brought**

   C Change *scenes* to **sceans**

   D Change the question mark to a period

6 What is the BEST way to combine sentences 16 and 17?

   F Observe the dramatic waterfalls and photograph the fascinating wildlife.

   G Observe and photograph the dramatic waterfalls and the fascinating wildlife.

   H Observe, photograph the dramatic waterfalls and the fascinating wildlife.

   J Observe the dramatic waterfalls, photograph the fascinating wildlife.

7 Which sentence does NOT belong in this paper?

   A Sentence 3

   B Sentence 5

   C Sentence 9

   D Sentence 12

GO ON

> **Read the introduction and the passage that follows it. Then read each question. Mark your answers on the Answer Document.**

Juan wrote a story about an event he'll remember for a long time. Read Juan's rough draft and think about the changes he needs to make. Then answer the questions that follow.

Books for All

(1) An article in the newspaper I read about our town library's limited availability of children's books. (2) This immediately caused me concern, as reading is one of my favorite pastimes. (3) I had already read my own books several times, so what would I do this summer with few books available to read? (4) Reading is one of my favorite pastimes. (5) That's when the idea occurred to me: I could start a book exchange! (6) I placed a few phone calls and soon had my friends on-board, ready to help me implement a plan.

(7) Collaborating with our town's library, we organized a community book exchange. (8) My friends and I posted notices about the exchange around town, inviting all children to bring books to the library to trade. (9) The next Saturday morning, a line of over 50 children and their parents stand outside the library!

GO ON

(10) My friends and I got to work immediately. (11) In a spare room in the library, we collected the books, distributing to people a ticket for each book they were exchanging. (12) Once the books assembled, a person could redeem a ticket for a book. (13) While the exchangers waited and chatted about their favorite books, my friends and I organized the books on shelfs according to genre and age-appropriateness. (14) By the end of the day, more than 200 people had passed through, but they all left with books to read over the summer.

(15) A parent of one of the children who attended happened to be a reporter for the local newspaper. (16) She was so impressed with our efforts that she took our picture and wrote an article about us. (17) I was proud that I was able to help my fellow book lovers, and I was happy to have new storys to read! (18) I will save the article in a scrapbook and use it to inspire other kids to find ways to help their communities.

Name _____ Date _____

8 What is the BEST way to revise sentence 1?

F I read an article in the newspaper about our town library's limited availability of children's books.

G An article in the newspaper about our town library's limited availability of children's books I read.

H I read in the newspaper, article, about our town library's limited availability of children's books.

J An article I read in the newspaper about our town library's limited availability of children's books.

9 What change should be made in sentence 9?

A Delete the comma after *Saturday*

B Change *line* to **lines**

C Insert a comma after *children*

D Change *stand* to **stood**

10 What change should be made in sentence 12?

F Change *books* to **book**

G Insert **were** before *assembled*

H Change *redeem* to **redeemed**

J Insert a comma after *ticket*

11 What change should be made in sentence 13?

A Change *chatted* to **chatting**

B Change *organized* to **organised**

C Change *shelfs* to **shelves**

D Change the period to an exclamation point

12 What revision is needed in sentence 14?

F Change *had passed* to **passing**

G Delete the comma after *through*

H Change *but* to **and**

J Change *left* to **leaving**

13 What change should be made in sentence 17?

A Change *was proud* to **were proud**

B Change *my* to **mine**

C Change *and* to **but**

D Change *storys* to **stories**

14 Which sentence does NOT belong in this paper?

F Sentence 4

G Sentence 8

H Sentence 11

J Sentence 16

GO ON

Read the introduction and the passage that follows it. Then read each question. Mark your answers on the Answer Document.

Kathryn wrote a book report about a new book she read. She wants you to read her book report and help correct it. When you finish reading, answer the questions that follow.

A Gem of a Story

(1) <u>Discovering the Shore</u>, published by Gold Leaf Books, is a new work of fiction by Charlene Burkett. (2) The book takes place on the Texas Gulf Coast. (3) It follows the main character, Matt, so that he discovers life by the sea.

(4) The book begins as Matt travels from his home in the Texas Panhandle to the Texas Coast to visit his grandmother. (5) During the long car ride, he makes it clear to Matt's parents that he would have preferred to spend summer vacation at home.

(6) Once him arrives at the coast, Matt's mood begins to change little by little. (7) Having never been to the beach before, Matt is slowly charmed by the sound of the waves and the sea. (8) On peaceful walks, at sunset, he and Grandma have heartfelt comversations. (9) On one walk, swimming only a few yards away from the shore, Grandma points out

dolphins. (10) By the end of the summer, Matt is hesitant to return home.

(11) He has a new admiration for his grandmother and he has discovered

a love for the ocean.

(12) Burkett's writing is descriptive, especially when she portrays

life by the ocean's shore. (13) The plot is moving and the characters are

realistic. (14) Readers will grow to love the coast just as Matt does, and

they will cheer as he grows closer to his grandmother. (15) Burkett has

given a sparkling gem of a story!

15 What change should be made in sentence 3?

   A Change *follows* to **was following**

   B Change *character* to **charactar**

   C Change *so that* to **while**

   D Change *sea* to **Sea**

16 What change should be made in sentence 5?

   F Delete the comma after *ride*

   G Change *Matt's* to **his**

   H Change *preferred* to **prefered**

   J Change *spend* to **spending**

17 What revision should be made in sentence 6?

   A Change *him* to **he**

   B Change *arrives* to **had arrived**

   C Change *Matt's* to **Matts'**

   D Change the period to an exclamation point

18 What change, if any, should be made in sentence 8?

   F Delete the comma after *walks*

   G Change *have* to **has**

   H Change *comversations* to **conversations**

   J Make no change

GO ON

19 What is the BEST way to revise sentence 9?

A Swimming dolphins Grandma points out on one walk, only a few yards away from the shore.

B On one walk, dolphins Grandma points out swimming only a few yards away from the shore.

C Swimming only a few yards away from the shore, on one walk Grandma points out dolphins.

D On one walk, Grandma points out dolphins swimming only a few yards away from the shore.

20 What change should be made in sentence 11?

F Change *admiration* to **admirion**

G Insert a comma after *grandmother*

H Change *love* to **loves**

J Change *ocean* to **Ocean**

21 What change should be made in sentence 15?

A Change *has* to **had**

B Insert **us** after *given*

C Change *sparkling* to **sparkleing**

D Change the exclamation point to a question mark

BE SURE TO MARK YOUR ANSWERS ON THE ANSWER DOCUMENT.

Writing: Written Composition

> Write a personal narrative about a positive
> experience you have had.

Use a separate sheet of paper to plan your composition. Then write it on the lined
pages that follow.

The information in the box below will help you remember what you should think about
when you write your composition.

> REMEMBER—YOU SHOULD
>
> ❑ write about a positive experience you
>   have had
>
> ❑ use the first-person point of view
>
> ❑ use an interesting opening to grab the
>   reader's attention
>
> ❑ include details about the most
>   important events and present them in
>   the order in which they took place
>
> ❑ try to use correct spelling,
>   capitalization, punctuation, grammar,
>   and complete sentences

Name _____ Date _____

_____

_____

_____

_____

_____

_____

_____

_____

_____

_____

_____

_____

_____

_____

_____

_____

Name _____ Date _____

Reading

An Ancient People

1   Over the years, scientists have unearthed many exciting secrets of an ancient people. Clues left behind show that these people were advanced in many fields. They built <u>majestic</u> pyramids and huge cities. They developed a system of numbers and a written language. Through art and writing, they left records of their history. The tombs of their kings were filled with <u>priceless treasures</u> for use in the afterlife. In many ways, this civilization was similar to that of the Ancient Egyptians, but it was a world away. This was the civilization of the Ancient Mayas in Central America.

Pyramids

2   Mayans built pyramids in many parts of Central America. Like all pyramids, they are large at the bottom and small at the top. Unlike Egyptian pyramids, the Mayan structures have sides like the steps of a staircase. While the steps are too steep to be used as stairs, they may have had other purposes. The pattern of steps on one pyramid seems to represent the seasons and the days of the year. Shadows cast on the steps change throughout the year. These changes show the movement of the sun through the seasons. The Mayans designed the pyramid so that it gives a <u>remarkable</u> sign twice a year. It happens only when the sun is directly overhead at the equator. On those days, the shadow of a snake appears to climb or descend the steps!

3   Pyramids were at the heart of every Mayan city. They stood up to twenty stories tall. Their towering presence was meant to serve as a reminder of the greatness of Mayan rulers.

GO ON ➡

Calendars

4   The Mayans excelled in astronomy and math. They invented a number system based on the number twenty. The Mayans had the <u>distinction</u> of using the concept of zero long before most other cultures did. Mayans charted the movements of objects in the night sky in great detail. They came to understand that the movements were <u>cyclical</u>. This knowledge led them to create <u>elaborate</u> calendars. The calendars plotted the movement of stars and planets with great accuracy. In fact, they can still be used today to predict the dates of eclipses!

Writing

5   The Mayans developed one of the earliest written languages. Their writings have been found on stone tablets and pottery. They also wrote in books made of tree bark, but most of the books have been lost. Like the Egyptians, Mayans used pictures as letters. The letters are part of a complex system of writing. For a long time, it was too hard for experts to understand. That is because some symbols stand for a whole word while others stand for just one syllable. Also, the symbols to spell a word can be arranged in different ways. In recent years, experts have finally broken the code, and they can now read the Mayan writings. Most praise Mayan kings and their belief in many gods or tell highlights of Mayan history.

Art

6   The Mayans used art to show respect for their gods and rulers. Likenesses of these figures were carved in stone high on buildings. Their stone faces are mysterious and commanding. Thrones carved of stone often showed the king sitting with gods. Some carvings show rulers with their heirs or ancestors. Others <u>depict</u> them waging war or conquering enemies. The king's daily life was also shown in art. Scenes painted on pots show kings at feasts and celebrations.

7   Mayans believed art and beauty were important in the afterlife. For that reason, they placed fine works of art in tombs. Statues, jade masks, and jewelry are among the artworks found in Mayan tombs.

8   Recently, carvings and statues have been discovered in underground temples, too. The temples are built in a <u>labyrinth</u> of caves. Experts wonder whether the Mayans used the temples as burial places. That is just one of the mysteries of the Mayans that is still waiting to be solved!

GO ON

1 What is the main idea of paragraph 1?

  A The Mayans built large pyramids and cities in ancient times.

  B The Mayans built a great civilization similar to that of the Ancient Egyptians.

  C Scientists have found clues that show that the Mayans had a written language.

  D The Mayans believed the treasures they put in tombs would be used in the afterlife.

2 What does the word <u>majestic</u> mean in paragraph 1?

  F Splendid

  G Puzzling

  H Simple

  J Unusual

3 What does the word <u>priceless</u> mean in paragraph 1?

  A Without much value

  B Of unknown value

  C Having a secret price

  D Too valuable for a price

4 Mayan pyramids were different from Egyptian pyramids in that they were—

  F erected in ancient times

  G small, well-hidden structures

  H large at the bottom and small at the top

  J built with sides that looked like stair steps

5 Which fact supports the opinion that the Mayans liked to create dramatic effects with their structures?

  A They began using zero before most other cultures.

  B They used astronomy to help them create accurate calendars.

  C They created the illusion of a snake crawling on the pyramid steps.

  D They used some symbols to represent a whole word and others to represent one syllable.

6 Which word belongs to the same word family as the word <u>distinction</u> in paragraph 4?

  F Disclose

  G Distance

  H Distribute

  J Distinguish

7 What does the word <u>cyclical</u> mean in paragraph 4?

  A Rapid

  B Random

  C Repeating

  D Remarkable

8 What does the word <u>elaborate</u> mean in paragraph 4?

  F Beautiful

  G Complex

  H Delicate

  J Simple

GO ON

9   What similarity between Egyptian and Mayan writing is mentioned in the selection?

   A   Both use pictures as letters.

   B   Both are decorated by extra pictures.

   C   Both use one symbol for each syllable.

   D   Both have several spellings for the same word.

10   Which statement about Mayan art is an opinion expressed by the author?

   F   *Likenesses of these figures were carved in stone high on buildings.*

   G   *Their stone faces are mysterious and commanding.*

   H   *For that reason, they placed fine works of art in tombs.*

   J   *Recently, carvings and statues have been discovered in underground temples, too.*

11   What does the word <u>depict</u> mean in paragraph 6?

   A   Show

   B   Describe

   C   Entertain

   D   Imitate

12   Which sentence from the selection states the main idea of paragraph 6?

   F   *The Mayans used art to show respect for their gods and rulers.*

   G   *Some carvings show rulers with their heirs or ancestors.*

   H   *Thrones carved of stone often showed the king sitting with gods.*

   J   *The king's daily life was also shown in art.*

13   Which detail supports the idea that Mayans believed art was important in the afterlife?

   A   Mayan scribes added artwork to their writings.

   B   Mayan kings were buried with beautiful works of art.

   C   Mayans decorated pottery with pictures of the king's daily life.

   D   Mayans put stone likenesses of kings and gods on their buildings.

14   What does the word <u>labyrinth</u> mean in paragraph 8?

   F   Hole

   G   Maze

   H   Tunnel

   J   Temple

GO ON

15 Which word has the same sound as the underlined letter in trea<u>s</u>ure?

A fizzy

B unsure

C collision

D smashing

16 Which word has the same suffix as the word <u>remarkable</u>?

F label

G stable

H dabble

J likeable

17 What is the correct way to divide the word <u>burial</u> into syllables?

A bur • ial

B bur • i • al

C bu • ria • l

D bur • ia • l

GO ON

Read this selection. Then answer the questions that follow it.
Mark your answers on the Answer Document.

The Stonecutter's Wish

1   Long ago, there lived a stonecutter who made his living fashioning useful items out of rock. He chiseled everything from flat stepping stones to heavy blocks for building great houses. The stonecutter was never without customers because everyone valued his reliable skills and careful work.

2   One day, the stonecutter delivered stone blocks to the home of a wealthy family. The opulent home was filled with marvelous and beautiful things. Finest of all was the master's luxurious bed, with elaborate carvings on its headboard and sheets of silk on its plump feather mattress.

3   "If only I were rich and could sleep in such a bed," lamented the stonecutter. "I would be happier than anyone in the world!"

4   Day after day, the stonecutter daydreamed about the elegant possessions and life of a rich man. How he wished for that life! He pictured in vivid detail the mansion he would own if he were wealthy.

5   Then one day, a strange and astonishing thing happened. When he returned home from work, the stonecutter discovered his modest hut had disappeared, and in its place was a mansion just like the one in his daydreams!

6   "What a fortunate turn of events!" cried the stonecutter. He decided to give up his occupation to enjoy his newfound prosperity. At first he was content, sitting all day in his mansion, but in time he grew restless

and wandered outside to admire his gardens. The harsh summer sun burned his skin and made him feel faint. It blazed so intensely that the grounds around the mansion quickly became scorched and dried up.

7   The stonecutter pondered his situation. "I am wealthy and the sun hasn't a single penny," he thought. "Yet the sun can parch the life out of everything green. Its baking heat steals my strength and withers my will. If only I were the sun, I would be mightier than anything anywhere!"

8   The next morning another strange and astonishing thing happened. When the stonecutter awoke, he was no longer in his elegant bed in his elegant house. He was high above the Earth and was filled with a fiery feeling of power. The stonecutter had become the sun!

9   The stonecutter, fascinated by his new self, shone his piercing rays onto the Earth. Fields and crops shriveled under his wilting power. People of all kinds—young, old, rich, and poor—suffered in his heat. Their faces reddened, their strength faded, and they were forced to take shelter in their homes. The stonecutter felt no sympathy for them. Instead, he swelled with pride when he saw how everything on Earth became powerless before him. His pride lasted until one day when a soft, white cloud covered his face and gave the Earth relief. The sun had no power as long as the cloud floated in front of him.

10   "How is it that a cloud can stop my rays? There is no satisfaction in being the sun if I am not the greatest of all," he observed bitterly. "A cloud is the thing to be. If only I were a cloud, I would be greater than the sun. I would be greater than anything anywhere!"

11   When night came and the sun sank out of sight from the land, a third strange and astonishing thing happened. The stonecutter still appeared high above the Earth, but he no longer had the sun's fiery power. Instead, he drifted through the sky with a serene, silent kind of strength. When morning came, he saw his great shadow moving over the ground. The stonecutter had become the cloud!

12   Delighted at his transformation, the stonecutter puffed himself up larger and wider. He held back the sun's rays and sprinkled down rain to refresh everything below. His precipitation made the whole Earth green and lush again.

GO ON

13   The stonecutter wanted to see the extent of his power so he rained and stormed with all his might. Torrents of rain overflowed rivers and flooded the land. Towns, villages, and roads washed away. With satisfaction, the stonecutter surveyed the <u>destruction</u> he had caused. Then he noticed that one thing had remained <u>immovable</u> in the face of his violent storms. It was an immense rock on the side of the mountain.

14   "That rock is unaffected by my power though everything around it is flooded or destroyed!" cried the stonecutter in angry <u>disbelief</u>. "If only I were the rock, I would be stronger than the cloud and the sun. At last, I would be stronger than anything anywhere!"

15   The next morning, the stonecutter had a strange and astonishing feeling. He felt immense and solid and strong enough to withstand any assault. The stonecutter had become the rock!

16   He laughed at the blazing sun and the pelting rain because nothing moved or changed him in the slightest way. Then suddenly, something small and sharp cut into him and severed a large hunk of rock that fell to the ground. The attacker was a stonecutter working his trade! Though the rock had the strength to endure many things, its power was useless in resisting the hammer and chisel.

17   The stonecutter in the rock roared in indignation. "How is it that a mere man can destroy this mightiest of rocks? If only I were a stonecutter, I would be satisfied at last!"

18   Then a strange, but not so astonishing, thing happened. The stonecutter awoke in his own modest bed in his modest little hut. He went back to his trade and worked hard every day. Though he had very little, he had all that he needed. Instead of longing for power and greatness, the stonecutter was satisfied with his life for he was sure he was as happy as anyone anywhere.

18 The problems faced by the main character in this story are caused by—

   F   the stonecutter's lack of work

   G   the floods that wash out his town

   H   the character's own greed and envy

   J   the snobbishness of a rich customer

19 What does the word opulent mean in paragraph 2?

   A   Complicated

   B   Friendly

   C   Luxurious

   D   Sparkling

20 Which word belongs to the same word family as the word possessions in paragraph 4?

   F   Impossible

   G   Postcard

   H   Deposit

   J   Possessed

21 What does the word prosperity mean in paragraph 6?

   A   Career

   B   Dwelling

   C   Power

   D   Wealth

22 What makes the stonecutter become dissatisfied with being a rich man?

   F   The sun's heat

   G   His own boredom

   H   His garden's ugliness

   J   The flood's destruction

23 What does the word pondered mean in paragraph 7?

   A   Considered

   B   Explained

   C   Regretted

   D   Remembered

24 What does the word sympathy mean in paragraph 9?

   F   Joy

   G   Hatred

   H   Shame

   J   Understanding

25 What does the word powerless mean in paragraph 9?

   A   Full of power

   B   Against power

   C   Without power

   D   Having more power

GO ON

Name _____ Date _____

26 One similarity between the character's experience as the sun and his experience as a cloud is that in both roles he—

F makes fields and crops wilt

G enjoys using his power to help others

H does destructive things to prove his power

J tries to damage the rock on the mountainside

27 What happens when the stonecutter tests his power as a cloud?

A The Earth feels refreshed and green.

B The sun turns cold and stops shining.

C Floods wash away cities, towns, and roads.

D The huge rock slides down the mountainside.

28 What does the word <u>immovable</u> mean in paragraph 13?

F Moving inward

G Moving outward

H Constantly moving

J Not able to be moved

29 Why does the stonecutter laugh when he realizes he is a rock?

A He knows he is about to become a stonecutter again.

B He realizes he made a silly mistake because now he can't move.

C He feels smug because the sun and rain cannot move or change him.

D He thinks he has outsmarted the man with the hammer and chisel.

30 With each new form the stonecutter takes on, he—

F daydreams about being a rich man again

G grows more homesick for his modest hut

H recognizes and envies a different kind of power

J feels angry that he has to get used to a new life

31 Why is the last paragraph important?

A It describes the setting of the story.

B It introduces the main problem of the story.

C It explains the lesson learned by the main character.

D It describes a flashback to an event that happened earlier.

GO ON

32 The stonecutter had many customers because he was known for his careful work and his—

   F competent

   G competently

   H competence

   J competition

33 Which word has the same sounds as the underlined letters in fortunate?

   A water

   B created

   C delicately

   D eggbeater

34 Which word has the same sounds as the underlined letters in destruction?

   F sugar

   G fasten

   H instructing

   J pleasure

35 What is the base word for the word disbelief?

   A dis

   B bell

   C lie

   D belief

BE SURE TO MARK YOUR ANSWERS ON THE ANSWER DOCUMENT.

Writing: Revising and Editing

> Read the introduction and the passage that follows it. Then read each
> question. Mark your answers on the Answer Document.

*Brianna is writing a book report. She wants you to help her correct her rough
draft. As you read Brianna's book report, think about the changes she should
make to correct and improve it. Then answer the questions that follow.*

A Book for Pet Lovers

(1) *The Dog Quest* is the story of two kids who work really hardly to get

a dog. (2) The story begins with Jett and Laila begging their parents to let

them have a dog. (3) Their parents are hesitant to get a pet, though.

(4) They point out that it takes time, money, and effort to train and care for

a pet. (5) They also think a pet will cause extra messes before the house.

(6) Jett and Laila remain determined. (7) They do all they can

to address their parents' concerns. (8) First, they take on more

housecleaning chores. (9) Then, with their parents' permission and help,

they start a pet-care business. (10) They promise to use their profits to

help pay for dog food and vet bills.

(11) The problems Jett and Laila have in their pet business are the

funniest of the book. (12) They have some incredibble mishaps with Lars

the cowardly Great Dane, Boo the disappearing snake, and Chaos the

claw-happy cat.

(13) In the end, the parents change their minds. (14) They admit that Jett and Laila have prove they will take good care of a dog. (15) They all go to the animal shelter together to find just the right pet. (16) The kids use their pet-sitting experience to screen the dogs for bad habits.

(17) I think any one who likes animals and humorous fiction is sure to enjoy reading *The Dog Quest*.

---

1   What change should be made in sentence 1?

   A Change **Quest** to **quest**

   B Change **work** to **working**

   C Change **hardly** to **hard**

   D Change **get** to **got**

2   What change should be made in sentence 5?

   F Change **They** to **Them**

   G Change **will** to **was**

   H Change **before** to **around**

   J Insert a comma after **messes**

3   What change should be made in sentence 11?

   A Change **their** to **there**

   B Change **pet** to **pets'**

   C Change **are** to **be**

   D Insert **parts** after **funniest**

4   What change should be made in sentence 12?

   F Change **have** to **has**

   G Change **some** to **sum**

   H Change **incredibble** to **incredible**

   J Change **disappearing** to **disappearance**

GO ON

5 What change, if any, should be made in sentence 14?

A Change *admit* to **admits**

B Change *prove* to **proven**

C Change *good* to **well**

D Make no change

6 Which sentence could BEST be added after sentence 16?

F Your local animal shelter is a good place for to find a great pet.

G Dogs need attention and training in order to learn how to follow commands.

H They talk about the time that Boo the snake hid behind the books in a bookcase.

J Ultimately, they choose a great mixed-breed dog and make him part of their pet-sitting team.

7 What change should be made in sentence 17?

A Change *think* to **thinks**

B Change *any one* to **anyone**

C Insert a comma after *animals*

D Change *reading* to **reader**

> **Read the introduction and the passage that follows it. Then read each question. Mark your answers on the Answer Document.**

Steven wrote this narrative to tell about a field trip to a museum. He would like you to read his paper and suggest corrections and improvements he should make. When you finish reading, answer the questions that follow.

An Awe-Inspiring Field Trip

(1) Our class field trip to the Regional Museum of Culture was a big surprise to me. (2) I expected the exhibit about Ancient Egypt to be a little boring, but I was wrong. (3) It was one of the most fascinating things I have ever see!

(4) It didn't take long to figure out that this exhibit was something special.

(5) As soon as we walked the first room, we all gasped. (6) The room was

darkened except for little spotlights on shimmering artifacts spread around

the room. (7) The shimmering turned out to be the lights reflecting on gold!

(8) There were golden statues, earrings, bracelets, breastplates, and more.

(9) The most breathtaking artifact was a mask from a mummy. (10) The

mask looked like the face of a real person, except for its brillint golden skin!

(11) In the next room were more artifacts that had been buried with

royalty and other powerful Egyptians. (12) Many objects were decorated

with gems, delicate carvings, or painted designs. (13) These objects

showed the wealth the person with whom they were buried.

(14) Other artifacts from the tombs were personal items that the person

enjoyed in life. (15) There were hair combs, wigs, and make-up that both

men and women used. (16) A pair of sandals in the exhibit weren't much

different from the ones I like to wear in the summer. (17) They were wove

from plant fiber and still looked almost new! (18) There was even a wooden

board game that egyptian children used to play.

(19) Those everyday items were what interested me most. (20) I could

easily imagine Ancient Egyptians holding them and using them. (21) It

was awe-inspiring to be so close to things that were thousands of years

old. (22) It made me understand why historians can get excited about the

past. (23) History became my favorite subject!

GO ON

8 What change should be made in sentence 3?

   F Change *one* to **won**

   G Change *most* to **more**

   H Change *see* to **seen**

   J Change the exclamation point to a question mark

9 What change should be made in sentence 5?

   A Insert a comma after *soon*

   B Change *we* to **us**

   C Insert **into** after *walked*

   D Change *gasped* to **gasp**

10 What change should be made in sentence 10?

   F Change *real* to **reel**

   G Change *except* to **accept**

   H Change *its* to **it's**

   J Change *brillint* to **brilliant**

11 What change should be made in sentence 13?

   A Change *These* to **This**

   B Change *objects* to **object**

   C Change *showed* to **showing**

   D Insert **of** after *wealth*

12 What change should be made in sentence 17?

   F Change *wove* to **woven**

   G Insert a comma after *and*

   H Change *looked* to **looks**

   J Change *almost* to **allmost**

13 What change should be made in sentence 18?

   A Change *There* to **They're**

   B Change *board* to **bored**

   C Change *egyptian* to **Egyptian**

   D Change *used* to **use**

14 What is the BEST way to revise sentence 23?

   F Until then, history became my favorite subject!

   G As a result of that field trip, history became my favorite subject!

   H Do you know that history became my favorite subject?

   J On the other hand, history became my favorite subject!

Read the introduction and the passage that follows it. Then read each
question. Mark your answers on the Answer Document.

*Laura is writing a narrative about how a friend helped her at a track meet.
She would like you to read her first draft and suggest ways she can revise
and improve it. When you finish reading, answer the questions that follow.*

A Friend to the Rescue

(1) I'll never forget the day that Marisa and I became friends.

(2) She turned what could have been a dreadful day into a great one.

(3) It all happened at our annual track-and-field meet. (4) I am passionate
about running and I was signed up for two events—the four-hundred-yard
dash and a relay in which four team members each run one hundred yards.
(5) Everyone on my relay team was an exceptional runner, and we had high
hopes of win until the week before the event. (6) Our teammate Lisa injured
a muscle in one of her calfs and had to drop out of the race. (7) What would
take her place with the competition just days away?

(8) We soon found out. (9) During our training sessions, Marisa gave
her best effort and showed herself to be a tough competitor, though she
wasn't as fast as Lisa had been.

(10) On the day of the meet I lined up for the four-hundred-yard dash and noticed that Marisa was competing, too. (11) I didn't think I'd have any difficulty outrunning her. (12) However, as we passed the halfway mark, I was astonished to see that Marisa had taken the lead. (13) I tried to pull ahead, but I stumbled and fell. (14) From the opposite side of the track, Marisa saw me sprawled on the ground. (15) While the other runners sprinted toward the finish, Marisa stepped off the track and ran over to help me. (16) She was moments away from winning race and she sacrificed the blue ribbon to make sure I was okay.

(17) As Marisa helped me limp to the bleachers, the spectators cheered. (18) Our teammates were disappointed at the loss, but they understood what Marisa did. (19) Even though I hurt me and didn't win any races at that meet, I consider it my lucky day. (20) Marisa has been my best friend ever since.

GO ON

15 What change should be made in sentence 5?

   A Change *Everyone* to **Every one**

   B Change *exceptional* to **exception**

   C Change *win* to **winning**

   D Change *before* to **under**

16 What change should be made in sentence 6?

   F Change *injured* to **injures**

   G Change *her* to **hers**

   H Change *calfs* to **calves**

   J Change *had* to **has**

17 What change should be made in sentence 7?

   A Change *What* to **Who**

   B Change *take* to **took**

   C Change *with* to **inside**

   D Change the question mark to a period

18 Which sentence could BEST be added after sentence 8?

   F There was no chance of Lisa recovering in time for the meet.

   G With only days left to practice, we had to work harder than ever.

   H The coach assigned a new student named Marisa to take Lisa's place.

   J For weeks, we had been cooperating and improving our performance.

19 What change should be made in sentence 10?

   A Insert a comma after *meet*

   B Change *noticed* to **notice**

   C Change *competing* to **competed**

   D Change *too* to **to**

20 What change should be made in sentence 16?

   F Change *moments* to *momentarily*

   G Insert **that** after *winning*

   H Insert a comma after *ribbon*

   J Change the period to a question mark

21 What change should be made in sentence 19?

   A Change *though* to **thought**

   B Change *me* to **myself**

   C Change *any* to **no**

   D Change *my* to **mine**

BE SURE TO MARK YOUR ANSWERS ON THE ANSWER DOCUMENT.

Writing: Written Composition

> Write an essay to inform readers about two or
> three interesting things to do in your community.

Use a separate sheet of paper to plan your composition. Then write your composition
on the lined pages that follow.

The information in the box below will help you remember what you should think about
when you write your composition.

> REMEMBER—YOU SHOULD
> ❏ write to inform readers about two or
> three interesting things to do in your
> community
> ❏ state the topic in your introduction, and
> get the reader's attention
> ❏ explain the main ideas using supporting
> details
> ❏ summarize the ideas in a conclusion
> ❏ try to use correct spelling, capitalization,
> punctuation, grammar, and complete
> sentences

Name _____ Date _____

_____

_____

_____

_____

_____

_____

_____

_____

_____

_____

_____

_____

_____

_____

_____

_____

_____

_____

_____

_____

_____

_____

_____

_____

_____

Reading

Read this selection. Then answer the questions that follow it.
Mark your answers on the Answer Document.

Who Turned on the Faucet?

by Sarah E. Romanov
illustrated by Brian Biggs

1   You walk into the kitchen while someone is chopping onions. A cold wind hits you in the face when you turn a corner on the street. You fall off your bike and scrape your knee. You watch a sad movie with your friends. What do all of these things have in common? They can all turn on the faucets in your eyes, sending rivers of warm tears flowing down your cheeks! Your tears might embarrass you at times, but they're very important to your eyes.

2   Tear glands under your upper eyelids are responsible for making tears, which are made of water, proteins, hormones, and a special oil that helps protect your eyes. If you've ever tasted your tears, you know they're also salty.

3   As tears wash down over your eyeballs, they drain out through tear ducts—tiny tubes that run between your eyes and nose. Look in a mirror and pull down your lower eyelid a bit. Do you see a little hole in the corner near your nose? That's the opening of a tear duct. If your eyes are watering, those tear ducts keep the flow under control. But if you start to cry, the ducts can't drain the tears quickly enough so they overflow, running down your face. Because tear ducts connect your eyes and nose, when your eyes water and your nose gets runny, you grab a tissue and blow out . . . tears! That's right, those are tears that have drained from your eyes into your nose.

GO ON ➡

4   Shedding tears is your body's way of giving your eyes the protection and moisture they need. In fact, you constantly make just enough tears to make sure your eyes aren't too dry. Blinking coats the eyes with this special moisturizer, called continuous tears, all day long.

5   Other tears called reflex tears flow to protect your eyes from things that aren't supposed to be in them. That is why you get teary-eyed when it's windy. Your eyes know that wind can dry them out fast, so they do their best to keep things wet! And when a piece of sand or an eyelash gets into your eye, those faucets turn on full-force to wash the invader out. So why does just the smell of onions make your eyes water? It's not really the smell—when an onion is cut, it releases chemicals that irritate your eyes.

6   Emotional tears are the least understood kind of tears. They flow when you watch a sad movie, get angry with someone, are very afraid, or even receive exciting news that makes you happy. Sometimes just seeing someone crying can make you cry, even if you don't feel sad yourself. Some people cry easily, while others have a hard time shedding tears.

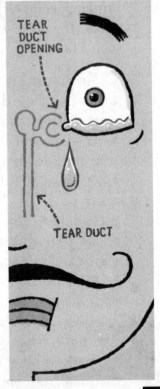

7   Among others, Dr. William Frey, a scientist from Minnesota, has spent many years studying tears. When Dr. Frey needed samples of tears to study, volunteers watched sad movies and collected their tears in little bottles for him. He discovered that emotional tears contain larger amounts of certain chemicals and hormones than the other types of tears do. Your body produces these substances in response to stress.

GO ON

8   When people are very stressed and have too many of these hormones and chemicals in their bodies, they can become sick, both physically and emotionally. Dr. Frey believes that shedding emotional tears releases these bad substances and helps maintain your body's proper chemical balance. This might explain why you feel better after a good cry.

9   There are still many mysteries about tears and crying that future research might explain. Scientists like Dr. Frey are working very hard to solve these mysteries. In the meantime, whenever you blink your eyes, smell freshly cut onions, or watch a sad movie, grab a tissue and be thankful for the wonderful way tears help take care of your body!

1   The author introduces the topic by—

   A   asking a series of questions about crying

   B   describing slicing an onion and shedding tears

   C   giving the dictionary definition of tears

   D   giving examples of times when people cry

2   Which kind of figurative language is used in this sentence?

   "They can turn on the faucets in your eyes, sending rivers of warm tears flowing down your cheeks!"

   F   Irony

   G   Personification

   H   Simile

   J   Metaphor

3   The three kinds of tears described in this article are—

   A   protein, hormone, and oil

   B   continuous, reflex, and emotional

   C   protective, moisturizing, and reactive

   D   balance, invasion, and stress

4   A reader can validly conclude from the article that—

   F   all tears are the same

   G   some people never shed tears

   H   tears are a part of good health

   J   all animals shed tears

5   How did Dr. Frey conduct his scientific research?

   A   He asked volunteers to watch sad movies.

   B   He chopped many onions.

   C   He read about tears.

   D   He studied stress in people.

GO ON

> **Read this selection. Then answer the questions that follow it.
> Mark your answers on the Answer Document.**

Friends Forever

June 15

Dear Chris,

1   Hello at long last from the Big Apple. I can't quite comprehend that I've been in New York this long without writing to you. I'm still not thrilled that we had to relocate here. For the first two whole weeks, nothing was unpacked, so it was like we were camping out in our own apartment. It took such a long time because our new apartment is so much smaller than our old house in San Francisco.

2   After unpacking, we spent a couple of weeks exploring our new neighborhood, which is really different from the one in San Francisco. Our apartment is in what's referred to as the East Village of Manhattan. There are no skyscrapers around here, just ancient brick apartment buildings, mostly four or five stories tall, with lots of little stores and interesting restaurants. Three blocks to the north is a park with a skatepark that I can't wait to try out, and right next to that is my future middle school, so I won't have to take a bus. It's strange because it looks similar to our old school—all brick and concrete with teeny tiny windows. I'm looking forward to showing you around.

Your friend,

Arnie

June 25

Dear Chris,

3   I've spent several days at the Metropolitan Museum, which is another reason why I haven't been able to write to you. The museum was the primary reason we had to move out here—it's where my mom works now. The building is absolutely enormous. There are so many exhibits to explore that I still haven't seen a quarter of them, and I've been there three times!

GO ON ➡

4   Once, while Mom was still working at the museum, Dad and I took an elevator to the observation deck of the Empire State Building. When we looked out, all we saw was the thickest fog you could ever imagine. Dad and I just stared at each other and laughed! Clearly, it's not only San Francisco that is famous for fog.

5   Another time, Dad and I ventured to see the barge and tanker traffic on the Hudson River. Later that same day, we met Mom in Central Park and went to see a Shakespearean play called Julius Caesar in an amphitheater there. So you can see, there's a lot to do around here.

Your friend,

Arnie

July 8

Dear Chris,

6   I'm now in my bedroom, which is so cramped and tiny that my bed and desk occupy almost all the floor space, leaving hardly any room to stretch out on the carpet the way I like to. My bed is next to a window, which looks out on the air conditioning vent that runs through the building, and when I lie down and concentrate, I can hear all sorts of interesting noises coming through the vents. Right now there's a lady singing the same opera song over and over. Last night, I heard chanting. There are several families from foreign countries that live in my building. I think I have heard at least three languages, not including English.

GO ON

7   Did I tell you that our building has its own doorman? Well, it does, and the doorman's son, Harvey, invited me to his house in Brooklyn. He's pretty normal, except that he's been studying karate since he was a toddler and goes to competitions with his dad in Japan! His dad has a twelfth degree black belt, and he teaches at the *dojo*, which is why Harvey's been practicing karate since he was two. The great news is that I'm going to their martial arts school starting next week.

8   We went up on the roof of our building the evening of the Fourth of July and had a perfect view of the fireworks, which they shoot off from a barge in the East River. Everyone in the building was up there with their friends, and people were barbecuing. It was really weird to watch from the top of the building instead of at a park, but I think I could get used to it. The fireworks display was intense and the barbecue was delicious.

9   I can't wait until you arrive—four weeks seems like forever. There are so many interesting places that I want to introduce you to, and you'll have to meet Harvey and the three brothers who live just down the hall. We'll definitely all have to go to the skatepark.

Your friend,

Arnie

6   In each of his three letters, Arnie describes—

   F   how much he misses Chris

   G   what he will do in the future

   H   his past in San Francisco

   J   events of the recent past

7   How does the author give the reader an idea of what Arnie is like?

   A   His letters have a realistic voice.

   B   His parents talk about him.

   C   His looks are given in great detail.

   D   His family history is very ordinary.

8   The reader learns from his letters that Arnie is—

   F   serious

   G   observant

   H   artistic

   J   lazy

9   In the first paragraph, Arnie contrasts—

   A   his old and new schools

   B   his old and new neighborhoods

   C   his old and new apartments

   D   the East Village and Manhattan

10   What can the reader conclude from paragraph 9?

   F   Arnie wishes Chris's family would move to New York, too.

   G   Arnie wishes Chris's family would not move to New York.

   H   Arnie misses Chris, but he is happy about his move to New York.

   J   Arnie misses Chris, and wishes his family had not moved.

GO ON

> **Read this selection. Then answer the questions that follow it.**
> **Mark your answers on the Answer Document.**

Watch Out!

as told by Joe Hayes
illustrated by Vicki Trego Hill

1   Once a poor couple struggled together to make a living from a tiny farm. They were a hard-working people, but their farm was so small and the soil was so poor that they were never able to get ahead. Each winter they ended up eating the seed for the next year's crop, and each spring they had to go to the money-lender in the village and borrow money to buy seeds so that they could plant again.

2   And then all year long they had to worry whether they would make enough to pay back the debt. Some years they were forced to be late in their payments, and then the money-lender would torment them with threats to take their small farm away from them.

3   Finally the year they had dreaded for so long arrived. Between hail in June and grasshoppers in August, hardly enough remained of their crop at harvest time to keep them alive through the winter. There was nothing left over to sell for cash to pay back the money-lender.

4   The poor couple didn't know what to do. Each time they went to the village, they carefully avoided the money-lender's house for fear that he would rush out and demand payment of them. Each day they watched the road in front of their farm nervously, sure that this was the day the money-lender would arrive to take their land away from them.

5   And then one Sunday, as they were leaving the village church and starting for home, the couple met up face to face with the money-lender in the center of the village plaza. Just as they had expected, the money-lender immediately demanded payment. "My money is long overdue," he told them. "If you don't pay me this very day, tomorrow I will take possession of your farm."

6   The poor people pleaded with the money-lender. "Please," they said, "take pity on us. It has been a very bad year, as you know. Next year we'll pay you double."

7   "Take pity?" the money-lender said scornfully. "Haven't I overlooked your late payments year after year? But now you've gone too far. I must have my money immediately, or your farm is mine."

8   Of course, the plaza was crowded with people leaving the church, and they soon began to notice the discussion between the couple and the money-lender. They gathered around to listen.

9   The money-lender noticed the crowd around them and began to grow uncomfortable. He didn't want to appear too hard-hearted. If he did, people might be too frightened to borrow money from him in the future.

10   "Very well," the money-lender told the farmer, "Let it never be said that I am unwilling to give people every possible opportunity. And besides, I'm in a playful mood this morning. I'll give you a chance to

be free from your debt. Do you see how the ground here in the plaza is covered with pebbles, some white, some black? I will pick up one pebble of each color and hold them in my closed fist. You may reach a finger in and pull out one pebble. If the pebble is black, your debt will be forgiven. You will owe me nothing. If the pebble you choose is white, your farm is mine this day."

11   The poor farmer had no choice but to agree, although he didn't really trust the money-lender to keep his word. The farmer and his wife watched as the money-lender knelt down and picked up two pebbles from the ground. No one else caught it, but the husband and wife saw that the money-lender had actually picked up two white pebbles. But they couldn't say anything because they knew the money-lender would just pretend to be insulted and throw the pebbles back into the ground and withdraw his offer.

12   "Are you ready?" asked the money-lender, with a sly smile on his face. He held out his hand with the fingers closed tightly over the two pebbles.

13   Filled with despair, the farmer reached toward the money-lender's hands, but his wife stopped him. "Wait!" she told him. "Let me choose. This feels like my lucky day."

14   The farmer quickly agreed, and the woman closed her eyes as if she were concentrating deeply. She took several deep breaths, and then reached out slowly toward the money-lender's closed fist. She seemed to be trembling with nervousness. She pried the fingers open and withdrew one pebble. And then she seemed to tremble even more violently. And she dropped the pebble! A gasp went up from the crowd.

15   "Oh, no!" cried the woman. "How clumsy of me!" But then she said to the money-lender, "Oh, well. It doesn't matter. There were only two colors of pebbles. Show us which color is left in your hand. The one I dropped had to be the other color."

16   "You're right," said everyone in the crowd, and they all told the money-lender, "Show us which color is left."

17   Grudgingly the money-lender opened his fist. "It's white!" everyone cried. "The one the woman chose had to be black." And they all began to congratulate the couple.

18   The money-lender forced a smile and shook the farmer's hand. "Congratulations," he said. And to the woman he added, "So this really was your lucky day. But take my advice, both of you. In the future, watch out that you don't get yourselves into such a position again."

19   "We will," said the farmer, smiling broadly. "And you, sir, in the future, watch out for clever women!"

20   The people in the crowd didn't quite know what the farmer was referring to, but the money-lender knew exactly what he meant, and he walked away grumbling to himself.

---

11   Which of the following events happens first?

   A   People in the plaza gather around a discussion.

   B   The poor couple offers to pay double the following year.

   C   The money-lender frees the couple from their debt.

   D   The money-lender demands his payment.

12   Which word describes the money-lender in this folktale?

   F   Nervous

   G   Violent

   H   Sneaky

   J   Foolish

13   The money-lender offers the poor couple a chance to wipe out their debt to—

   A   protect the future of his business

   B   get double his payment from them

   C   cheat them out of their farm

   D   persuade the woman to work for him

14   Which sentence best expresses the story's theme?

   F   Being clever and observant can save you.

   G   Lending money will get you into trouble.

   H   Always beware of crowds in open places.

   J   Always go with your second guess.

15   The poor woman is considered "clever" because she—

   A   saw what the money lender did and tricked him at his own game

   B   correctly guessed which hand the white pebble was in

   C   watched which hand the money lender put the white pebble in

   D   learned the lesson never to borrow money again

16   The story is told by—

   F   the poor woman

   G   a narrator observing the action

   H   the money-lender

   J   one of the people in the village

> **Read this selection. Then answer the questions that follow it.**
> **Mark your answers on the Answer Document.**

Public Libraries

1   Many towns across the United States have public libraries, places where people can borrow books, movies, or CDs. Children can listen to stories or participate in summer reading programs, and adults can take computer classes or take part in book discussions. These libraries are called public for several reasons. First, these services are provided for the public. Second, the services provided by the libraries cost money, which comes from the public. Third, libraries grew out of the actions of ordinary people who saw that there was a need to educate people and came together to find a way to meet that need.

2   One of the earlier libraries in the United States was started by Benjamin Franklin. In the early days of the nation, books were expensive and hard to find, so Franklin decided to form a group of people who would pool their money to purchase books. He created a subscription library. These subscription libraries started appearing throughout the country but were available only to members who paid a yearly fee, or subscription, for the right to borrow books.

3   In the mid-1800s, women formed literary societies, or reading groups. At that time, women did not get the same education as men; in order to educate themselves, and each other, they formed groups. The literary societies they formed would share and discuss books to increase their knowledge about the world.

4   As these societies grew, women realized the education gained from books should be accessible to everyone, not just those who could afford the yearly subscription fee. They started to create their own libraries.

These libraries started as library associations, whose missions were to make books accessible. Library associations accomplished that by taking over existing subscription libraries, raising money to buy books, and collecting donations of book collections from citizens. Though these libraries started small, their collections grew and they became popular. It wasn't necessary to purchase a subscription for these libraries, so more and more people were able to access the books in the collections.

5   As these libraries grew, two new problems arose and the societies turned to the public to help solve them. First, the collections grew too big to fit in existing buildings. As a result, some associations raised money from the community to purchase new buildings. In other communities, buildings that could serve as libraries were donated by wealthy citizens. Second, the societies could not raise enough money to cover the cost of running the libraries. They realized that the government could help with those costs. By 1900, most libraries were supported by the public with tax money.

6   Libraries grew out of the idea that people should have a chance to better themselves through education. Giving the public access to books through libraries was one way to address this goal. When the public took over running libraries, through their tax dollars, libraries truly became public in all senses of the word. Many libraries still in existence today in the United States owe their start to a small group of local people who planted the seed of the wonderful library that the public continues to enjoy.

1638—The oldest library in the United States was founded, becoming the Harvard University Library.

1731—A subscription library association, The Library Company of Philadelphia, was founded by Benjamin Franklin.

1849—The New York Public Library started.

1854—Boston Public Library opened to the public on March 20. It was the first to be supported by direct public taxation.

GO ON

17 Literary societies formed in the 1800s to—

A encourage children to read

B support schools which needed books

C provide money for public libraries

D provide education for women

18 The timeline shows—

F why Benjamin Franklin invented a library

G public libraries over two hundred years

H why public libraries were started in New England

J how public libraries were started by women in small communities

19 Based on the article, what judgment can the reader make about public libraries?

A They are an example of community action.

B They serve children more than adults.

C They are quiet places where one can study.

D They hold more books than school libraries.

20 How were subscription libraries different from today's public libraries?

F Only adult men could use subscription libraries.

G Subscription libraries held magazines but not books.

H Subscription libraries only served populations in large cities.

J Borrowers paid money to use subscription libraries.

21 In the last paragraph, the author compares public libraries to a—

A seed that grows over time

B garage where items are stored

C cupboard full of nourishing food

D building built brick by brick

GO ON

Read this selection. Then answer the questions that follow it.
Mark your answers on the Answer Document.

Limber Wood and Shallow Roots

1 It was April, and the wind howled like a hungry coyote as a storm approached. Jasper's Uncle Ken, his mother's brother, was visiting to install new brakes on the family car. "Wind's coming up," Ken mumbled as he came into the house, chewing a toothpick and wiping his hands on an oil-stained bandana.

2 The door slammed violently behind him, and Ken and his sister exchanged knowing glances. Rain pelted the windows and the roof, sounding like horses running wild, while the wind howled as though it would like to tear the house apart. Jasper's mother threw sand into the stove, extinguishing the fire, and the three of them walked outside to take shelter in the root cellar. Clinging to each other to avoid being blown away by the persistent wind, they fought to walk the handful of steps from the door to the cellar. Ken struggled with the door, and with a mighty heave, wrenched it open. Jasper and his mother scrambled quickly inside.

3 Once inside, Jasper and Ken crouched in a corner, while Jasper's mother found the blankets that they kept in the cellar along with water and food in case of emergencies like this. She also found the

small battery-powered radio. Turning it on, she learned that the winds had reached over seventy-five miles per hour. After that, the radio kept replaying the high-pitched tone indicating that there was an emergency. The announcer said where tornadoes had been sighted, and where they had touched down.

4   Suddenly, over the radio signal, they heard a new sound: a rhythmic creaking followed by a long, low moan, like a bellowing cow. Seconds later, the first tree hit the roof, toppling the chimney. They could smell the soot from the inside of the chimney, and Jasper's mother reached for him.

5   As they sat huddled in the cellar waiting out the storm, they heard at least a dozen more trees give in to the wind. They heard the roots let go with that same eerie groan, and then the pines hit the roof—almost gently—since their bendable trunks didn't break and their shallow roots let them easily pull away from the earth. Finally, an hour after it began, the storm lessened, the trees stopped creaking, and the radio started playing music again and relaying optimistic news.

6   They emerged from the cellar to blue skies with fluffy white clouds and clean-washed air. Branches were everywhere and half a dozen trees leaned on the roof, but miraculously no windows had been broken. Jasper and his mother just stood there, gaping at the way the trees almost seemed to caress the outside walls of the house. "Wow," Jasper finally whispered as they stepped over trunks and branches, "We were lucky, weren't we?"

7   "We *are* lucky," his mother replied. "All that's broken is the chimney, and that can be repaired easily. We're lucky those trees are pines—limber wood and shallow roots probably saved our windows and our roof."

GO ON

Name _____ Date _____

22 Based on this story, which judgment can the reader make about tornadoes?

   F They can uproot trees and damage houses.

   G They last from five to twenty minutes.

   H They are formed when warm air meets cold air.

   J They are the most destructive force on earth.

23 The writer compares the wind to—

   A limber wood and shallow roots

   B horses running wild

   C a hungry howling animal

   D a tornado touching down

24 According to the story, which trees would be most dangerous in high winds?

   F Limber trees with shallow roots

   G Pines trees with many needles

   H Tall trees with many branches

   J Hardwood trees with deep roots

25 The best source to use to learn more about how fast the biggest tornadoes can spin is—

   A an atlas of the United States

   B a movie review

   C a novel about growing up in Kansas

   D an online encyclopedia

26 Which detail shows that Jasper's mother is well-organized?

   F She keeps blankets, water, food, and a radio in the root cellar.

   G She asks her brother to install new brakes on her car.

   H She knows that pines have shallow roots and limber wood.

   J She says that they are lucky when she sees the damage.

27 How much time passes during this story?

   A A minute

   B A few hours

   C Two days

   D One week

GO ON

> **Read this selection. Then answer the questions that follow it.**
> **Mark your answers on the Answer Document.**

EMU

1   An EMU is an Extravehicular Mobility Unit, a special kind of spacesuit used by astronauts while they are in space. "Extravehicular" means that they are used outside a space shuttle, a space station, or the vehicle. "Mobility" means that the suits let astronauts move around easily. They can even use their hands and fingers to perform fine motor tasks, such as repairing the space station. "Unit" means that although there are thousands of pieces and parts to these suits, they all function together to protect astronauts from space.

2   Space is a hostile place for people. In the dark, temperatures can reach 150 degrees below zero. In direct sunlight, the thermometer can hit 250 degrees. Both of these temperatures are more extreme than anything found on Earth. Space lacks air pressure and contains high levels of radiation. Tiny meteoroids, old satellites, and even trash constantly zoom through the airless void.

3   An EMU does not depend on support from a space station or shuttle. Astronauts carry PLSS on their backs. PLSS stands for Portable Life Support Systems. They provide oxygen, water, and temperature and air pressure control. With them, astronauts can work outside for up to nine hours at a time.

4   EMUs are reusable. The pieces come from many standardized parts. These can be fitted together in different ways to fit different astronauts. Somewhere, there is a huge closet of EMU parts: torsos and boots, gloves and helmets. The parts fit ninety percent of the population, and both men and women can wear them.

5   Astronauts do not wear the EMU inside the space station or shuttle. In order to go on a spacewalk, the astronauts must put the sections on in order.

    1. Put on the underlayer. This is similar to long underwear but with tubes that help cool the suit.

Name _____ Date _____

2. Enter the airlock area, where the rest of the EMU will be put on.

3. Attach the communication equipment, life support system, and arms to the EMU.

4. Rub antifog goo onto the visor, so it remains clear.

5. Attach a mirror and checklist to the sleeves of the EMU. Place a food bar and drink bag inside for easy access.

6. Check the lights and cameras to make sure they work. Place the visor on the helmet. Connect the communications equipment. Check to make sure that the communications equipment works.

7. Step into the lower part of the EMU, which extends above the waist.

8. Wiggle into the upper torso part. Attach the cooling tubes of the EMU into the life-support system. Attach the electricity to the life-support system.

9. Lock the lower part into the upper part of the EMU. Lock on the helmet.

10. Slip on the inner comfort gloves. Lock on the outer gloves.

6   After the EMU is on, the astronaut must check for leaks. If there are no leaks, the astronaut can leave the airlock and enter space. For the next nine hours, the EMU is like the astronaut's own personal spacecraft. When the spacewalk is finished, all the steps are done, but in reverse. When completed, the astronaut can once again enter the shuttle or space station.

GO ON ➡

28 Which details from the article support the need for EMUs?

    F Definitions of the initials

    G Facts about who can wear an EMU

    H Steps in putting on an EMU

    J Facts about the harshness of space

29 In paragraph 3, the author writes that the PLSS "provides oxygen, water, and temperature and air pressure control." The reader can conclude from this that—

    A astronauts can work outside the space station for up to nine hours

    B the Portable Life Support Systems are not essential to astronauts

    C humans need oxygen, water, and a certain temperature and air pressure to survive

    D astronauts in space need more oxygen and water than people on earth

30 The author compares—

    F an EMU to a normal set of clothes

    G an EMU to a personal spacecraft

    H components to standardized parts

    J men who wear EMUs to women who wear EMUs

31 Which statement is supported by information in the article?

    A When putting on an EMU, it is okay to perform the steps in any order.

    B If the spacewalk is short, there is no need to put on the EMU's underlayer.

    C Putting on an EMU takes a long time, but it is crucial to do every step in order.

    D Putting on an EMU takes a long time, and sometimes it is okay to skip a step.

32 The way to find out who makes EMUs would be to—

    F enter "EMU" or "spacesuit" in an online search engine

    G look up "space vehicles" in an encyclopedia

    H look up "spacesuits" in the yellow pages of the phone book

    J ask an adult who is interested in space travel

BE SURE TO MARK YOUR ANSWERS ON THE ANSWER DOCUMENT.

STOP

Name _____ Date _____

Writing: Revising and Editing

Read the introduction and the passage that follows it. Then read each question. Mark your answers on the Answer Document.

After visiting the Statue of Liberty, Maria wrote a report about it. Read Maria's report and think about changes she needs to make. When you finish reading, answer the questions that follow.

A View from the Top

(1) Standing 305 feet tall in New York Harbor, the Statue of Liberty is a majestic symbol of the United States. (2) Maybe you have seen pictures of the statue wearing a spiked crown and holding a torch. (3) During a Fourth of July celebration, I was honored to be one of 240 people who went inside the statue's crown. (4) We also visited an art museum that day.

(5) At ground level, ten people at a time entered into the base of the statue's pedestal. (6) Here I got to see the statue's original torch. (7) I got to photograph it. (8) The torch had been replaced long ago and then put on display. (9) Much taller than a person, the torch's enormity was absolutely shocking?

(10) Instead of taking an elevator to reach the top. (11) We had to climb 354 steps. (12) A spiral staircase of metal makes up the last 146 stairs. (13) Many of the steps are so narrow that the heel of my foot hung off the back, so I held tightly to the rail as a procaution. (14) It was a very much tiring climb.

(15) Once inside the crown, I was surprised at how small the space actually was. (16) Even though there were only ten people in the room, we had to stand side-by-side. (17) However, once I looked out one of the 25 windows, I quickly forgot the cramped space. (18) The breathtaking sight included the skylines of Brooklyn and Manhattan, bridges, and the setting sun reflecting off the water far below me.

(19) All too soon a park ranger told to begin the descent, it was time, but I won't soon forget my experience inside the crown of the Statue of Liberty.

1 What is the BEST way to combine sentences 6 and 7?

A Here I got to see and photograph the statue's original torch.

B The statue's original torch I got to see and photograph it here.

C Here I got to see, the statue's original torch, and here I got to photograph it.

D The statue's original, torch was here for me to see and for me to photograph.

2 What change should be made in sentence 9?

F Change *taller* to **tallest**

G Delete the comma after *person*

H Change *person* to **people**

J Change the question mark to an exclamation point

3 What revision is needed in sentences 10 and 11?

A Instead of taking an elevator to reach the top, and we had to climb 354 steps.

B Instead of taking an elevator to reach the top, we had to climb 354 steps.

C We had to climb 354 steps, and not taking an elevator to reach the top.

D Instead of taking the elevator to reach to top we climbed 354 steps instead.

4 What change should be made in sentence 13?

F Change *steps* to **step**

G Change *hung* to **hanged**

H Delete the comma after *back*

J Change *procaution* to **precaution**

5 What change should be made in sentence 14?

A Change *It* to **It's**

B Change *was* to **were**

C Change *very much tiring* to **strenuous**

D Change *climb* to **climbed**

6 What is the BEST way to revise sentence 19?

F All too soon we told a park ranger that we wanted to begin the descent, so I won't soon forget my experience inside the crown of the Statue of Liberty.

G All too soon a park ranger told us that it was time to begin the descent, but I won't soon forget my experience inside the crown of the Statue of Liberty.

H I won't soon forget my experience inside the crown of the Statue of Liberty, and all too soon us told a park ranger that it was time to begin the descent.

J Because it was time to begin the descent, an all too soon park ranger told us, I won't soon forget my experience inside the crown of the Statue of Liberty.

7 Which sentence does NOT belong in this paper?

A Sentence 1

B Sentence 4

C Sentence 12

D Sentence 17

Name _____ Date _____

*Avery wrote a story about a difficult decision she made recently. Read Avery's
rough draft and think about the changes she needs to make. Then answer the
questions that follow.*

Try New Things

(1) In the past, whenever someone would ask me what I liked to do,
I would always say, "I'm a gymnast." (2) My gymnastics career only
began when I was two years old, eleven years ago. (3) Growing up I spent
countless hours at the gym, practicing my skills. (4) Many of my friends
tried to convince me that I should try other things, such as softball or
tennis. (5) No one could appreciate my passion for the sport. (6) They
couldn't comprehend the thrill of pulling off a complicated move after
practicing it for months.

(7) Then shortly after my twelfth birthday something changed.
(8) Suddenly I didn't spend my day looking forward to working on the
balance beam, but competitions no longer excited me. (9) Instead some of
my teammates and me dreaded them. (10) What was happening?

(11) I wresled with my reluctance and persevered for a couple of months,

but I just grew more and more unhappy.

(12) To relieve my frustration, I started going to the track to run with my mother. (13) One day we were finishing our run when a woman approached us. (14) She introduced herself as the middle school track coach and invited me to come to practice the next day.

(15) That evening, I called my gymnastics coach, and she encouraged me to meet with the track team. (16) At track practice I were able to try new things. (17) I discovered that I was a fast runner, and my long jump was superb! (18) I ended up quitting the gymnastics team, but not the sport. (19) I still practice once a week, but I'm trying new things.

(20) People still ask me, "What's you're favorite thing to do?" (21) These days I smile and say, "I like to try new things."

---

8 What is the BEST way to revise sentence 2?

F When I was only two years old, my gymnastics career began eleven years ago.

G My gymnastics career when I was two years old began, only eleven years ago.

H When I was two years old, eleven years ago, my only gymnastics career began.

J My gymnastics career began eleven years ago, when I was only two years old.

9 What change should be made in sentence 7?

A Change *after* to **over**

B Change *my* to **mine**

C Insert a comma after *birthday*

D Change *something* to **Something**

10 What change should be made in sentence 8?

F Change *spend* to **spent**

G Delete the comma after *beam*

H Change *but* to **and**

J Change *me* to **I**

GO ON

11 What change, if any, should be made in sentence 9?

   A Change *Instead* to **Because**

   B Change *dreaded* to **dreded**

   C Change *me* to **I**

   D Make no change

12 What change should be made in sentence 11?

   F Change *wresled* to **wrestled**

   G Change *reluctance* to **reluctence**

   H Delete the comma after *months*

   J Change *but* to **so**

13 What change should be made in sentence 16?

   A Change *At* to **Under**

   B Change *practice* to **practicing**

   C Change *were* to **was**

   D Change *try* to **tried**

14 What change should be made in sentence 20?

   F Delete the comma after *me*

   G Change *you're* to **your**

   H Change *do* to **does**

   J Change the question mark to a period

GO ON

> **Read the introduction and the passage that follows it. Then read each question. Mark your answers on the Answer Document.**

Anna wrote a book report for school. Read her book report and think about corrections she should make. When you finish reading, answer the questions that follow.

First Flight

(1) I have always enjoying reading historical fiction. (2) I just finished reading *Seeing the First Flight* by Milton Nance. (3) It is a fantastick work of historical fiction. (4) In a new book, twelve-year-old Emily watches as Orville Wright makes the first airplane flight.

(5) Emily begins her story on the morning of the first flight. (6) Only a handful of people have gathered on the beach to witness history in the making. (7) Emily sees the Wright brothers flip a coin to determine who will attempt the first flight. (8) Orville, winning the coin toss, climbs onto the airplane. (9) Emily holds her breath as the plane lifts into the air for twelve seconds. (10) She watches it travel 120 feet. (11) The brothers then take turns flying the plane.

(12) Emily's thoughts are very much interesting. (13) She asks her if the airplane will transform the world. (14) She wonders if the american

Name _____ Date _____

people will ever use airplanes for travel. (15) Through her thoughts

and descriptions, readers catch a glimpse of the world into modern

transportation. (16) I felt inspired to imagine the future of travel.

---

15 What change, if any, should be made in sentence 1?

  A Change *have* to **had**

  B Change *enjoying* to **enjoyed**

  C Change *historical* to **Historical**

  D Make no change

16 What change should be made in sentence 3?

  F Change *is* to **be**

  G Change *fantastick* to **fantastic**

  H Change *of* to **or**

  J Change the period to a question mark

17 What change should be made in sentence 4?

  A Change *a* to **this**

  B Change *twelve-year-old* to **Twelve-year-old**

  C Change *watches* to **had watched**

  D Change *makes* to **making**

18 What change, if any, should be made in sentence 12?

  F Change *Emily's* to **Emilys**

  G Change *are* to **is**

  H Change *very much interesting* to **fascinating**

  J Make no change

19 What change should be made in sentence 13?

  A Change *She* to **Her**

  B Change *her* to **herself**

  C Change *transform* to **tramsform**

  D Change *world* to **World**

20 What change should be made in sentence 14?

  F Change *wonders* to **wondering**

  G Change *american* to **American**

  H Change *will ever use* to **had ever used**

  J Change the period to an exclamation point

21 What change should be made in sentence 15?

  A Change *thoughts* to **thinkings**

  B Delete the comma after *descriptions*

  C Change *catch* to **catched**

  D Change *into* to **before**

GO ON

Read the introduction and the passage that follows it. Then read each question. Mark your answers on the Answer Document.

Carlos wrote a story about a child who visits relatives in another country. Read Carlos's rough draft and think about the changes he needs to make. Then answer the questions that follow.

The Trip of a Lifetime

(1) Last summer, Adrian took a trip that most people only dream of taking. (2) He traveled to Germany with his parents to meet the family members he had only seen in pictures. (3) Adrian's parents came to the United States from Germany before Adrian was born. (4) I've been on a plane, but I've never traveled to Germany.

(5) The flight from the United States to Germany took more than ten hours. (6) Traveling by train from the airport, Adrian and his family reached they're relatives' home in the country in less than an hour. (7) Adrian's grandparents, aunts, uncles, and cousins were all waiting there, and they greeted Adrian as if they had known him all his life.

(8) The next day, the entire family went sightseeing in the Rhine River Valley. (9) The first stop was a castle that looked like it had been plucked from the pages of a fairy tale. (10) During a river cruise, the

GO ON

family saw many more castles, each with its own really very special

history. (11) That night, the family sat on the riverbank and witnessed a

magical fireworks show high above the water. (12) As his family watched

the fireworks, Adrian thought it was the more happier time of his life.

(13) Oh it would be difficult to say goodbye!

(14) Adrian and his parents look at pictures on the plane ride home

when Adrian suddenly exclaimed, "That was the trip of a lifetime!"

(15) When Papa asked which part of the trip was his favorite, Adrian

didn't hesitate to respond, "It was getting to spend time with our family.

---

22 What change should be made in sentence 6?

F Insert **While** before *Traveling*

G Delete the comma after *airport*

H Change *they're* to **their**

J Change *relatives'* to **relatives**

23 What change, if any, should be made in sentence 10?

A Delete the comma after *cruise*

B Change *saw* to **had seen**

C Change *really very special* to **unique**

D Make no change

24 What change should be made in sentence 12?

F Change *As* to **So**

G Change *watched* to **watches**

H Change *was* to **were**

J Change *more happier* to **happiest**

25 What change should be made in sentence 13?

A Insert a comma after *Oh*

B Change *difficult* to **difficulty**

C Change *say* to **said**

D Change the exclamation point to a question mark

26 What change, if any, should be made in sentence 14?

    F   Change *look* to **were looking**

    G   Change *when* to **while**

    H   Delete the comma after *exclaimed*

    J   Make no change

27 What change should be made in sentence 15?

    A   Change *asked* to **asks**

    B   Change *didn't* to **doesn't**

    C   Change *It* to **it**

    D   Insert a quotation mark after *family.*

28 Which sentence does NOT belong in this story?

    F   Sentence 1

    G   Sentence 4

    H   Sentence 7

    J   Sentence 11

BE SURE TO MARK YOUR ANSWERS ON THE ANSWER DOCUMENT.

Writing: Written Composition

Write an essay to persuade a friend to read your favorite book.

Use a separate sheet of paper to plan your composition. Then write your composition on the lined pages that follow.

The information in the box below will help you remember what you should think about when you write your composition.

REMEMBER, YOU SHOULD

❏ write to persuade a friend to read your favorite book
❏ state a clear goal or position in your introduction
❏ list facts and reasons to support your position
❏ use a positive and polite tone and respond to objections the reader may have
❏ try to use correct spelling, capitalization, punctuation, grammar, and complete sentences

Name _____ Date _____

_____

_____

_____

_____

_____

_____

_____

_____

_____

_____

_____

_____

_____

_____

Name _____ Date _____

_____

_____

_____

_____

_____

_____

_____

_____

_____

_____

_____

_____

_____

Reading

> **Read this selection. Then answer the questions that follow it.**
> **Mark your answers on the Answer Document.**

Project Frog

1   Cecilia spread out the money she had saved and counted it. She groaned, pretty sure that 63 dollars wouldn't save many frogs.

2   Cecilia's mother looked up from her work. "Are you thinking of buying something?" she asked.

3   "I'm trying to figure out <u>whether</u> or not I can help protect frogs," said Cecilia. "We learned in school that frogs around the world are dying. It's a huge problem. Unfortunately, my cash supply is anything *but* huge."

4   "Maybe you could pass out <u>informative</u> flyers to educate people about the issue," said her mom, trying to be <u>supportive</u>.

5   Cecilia considered the idea, but she wasn't sure that passing out flyers would get the kind of results she wanted. She wanted to do something interesting and <u>unique</u> to get people's attention. Cecilia was determined to take action and get other people to do the same. She headed to her computer in hopes of finding some inspiration. As she read article after article on the Internet, Cecilia took notes on what she learned about the frog problem:

6   • *The growing human population has led to more building and more pollution. Both can have fatal <u>consequences</u> for frogs.*

     • *Clearing of land and building new structures have destroyed much frog habitat.*

     • *Pesticides and weed killers used in farming can wash into streams and ponds where frogs live. Scientific data shows that these chemicals increase stress in frogs. That makes them less able to fight off disease.*

     • *A deadly skin fungus is wiping out frogs at an alarming rate. Scientists say that global warming has created <u>conditions</u> that allow the fungus to grow out of control.*

7   Finally Cecilia found a website that gave her a great idea.

GO ON

8   "Mom!" she said excitedly, "I know how to get people involved. I just need a few supplies from the hardware store and a couple of friends to help me build a model."

9   "A model of what?" asked her mother.

10   "Of this!" answered Cecilia. She handed her mother a printout with instructions for building a homemade wetland for frogs.

11   Her mother read the instructions and agreed that a homemade wetland would be a good way for Cecilia to use her limited resources. Her mom even offered to share the expenses. "But how will this mobilize other people?" she asked.

12   "We can pass out flyers to the neighbors advertising a class to be held in our backyard," said Cecilia. "People can see our model and learn how to do the same thing in their yard. It would not only help frogs but also look terrific!"

13   The next day, Cecilia and her mother bought the supplies. After Cecilia marked out the location for her backyard wetland, her friends helped her dig the hole. Her mom helped them install the plastic liner. Finally, they filled the pond with water and planted water lilies, grass, and ferns in and around the pond.

14   Cecilia thought the finished wetland looked like a great habitat for amphibians. She could hardly wait for the frogs to find it. In the meantime, she got to work making flyers and writing the project instructions she would explain in her class. She had the thrilling feeling that she was actually going to make a difference!

How to Create a Homemade Wetland

15   The simple steps below explain how you can create a great home for frogs that is also an attractive water feature for your yard.

Materials

16   Gather these items: rope or a garden hose, shovels, rocks of various sizes, several bags of sand, a plastic liner made specifically for ponds, water plants, ferns, grasses

Planning

17   First get your parents' permission to create a homemade wetland. Ask them for guidance in choosing the right place for the pond. Then use the rope or garden hose to mark the pond's shape and location. Remember that tadpoles cannot survive in full sun, so part of the pond should be shaded.

Site Preparation

18   Dig out the hole for your pond so that it has a shallow end and a deep end. The deepest part should go down about three feet. The other end should be shallow enough to stay muddy and bog-like. The sides should be gently sloped so amphibians can easily crawl in and out.

Building the Pond

19   Spread a layer of wet sand about two inches thick over the pond bottom. The sand will provide a cushion that protects the plastic pond liner from being punctured by rocks.

20   Inspect your pond liner thoroughly to make sure it doesn't have any holes. You must use a liner that is made especially for ponds because other kinds of plastic can break down and be toxic to wildlife.

21   Spread the liner over the sand, smooth it into place, and anchor it with rocks or bricks. Then bury the outer edges of the liner under six inches of soil. Add decorative pebbles and stones around the rim and fill the pond with water.

Planting

22   Let the pond water stand for three days to allow any chlorine to evaporate before you proceed with planting. Next, place large rocks and logs on the bottom of the pond and plant water lilies and other aquatic plants around them. Plants should cover more than half of the surface area of the pond. Having plenty of plants will slow the growth of algae and prevent your pond from becoming dirty or stagnant.

23   Along the muddy edge of the pond and in the shallow end of the pool, plant plenty of grasses and ferns where frogs can eat insects and lay eggs and where tadpoles can feed and hide.

Caution

24   Once your pond is ready, it may take a while for native frogs to discover it. Do not get impatient and buy frogs to add to your pond, or you could make frog decline worse! Frogs brought in from other places often eat native frogs and take over a local habitat.

---

1 Why was Cecilia frustrated at the beginning of the story?

A Her mother didn't understand what Cecilia's goal was.

B She couldn't find instructions for building a pond.

C Her school wasn't doing anything to protect frogs.

D She didn't have enough money to accomplish much.

2 Which word is a homophone for the word whether in paragraph 3?

F Waiter

G Weather

H Wherever

J Wither

3 What does the word informative mean in paragraph 4?

A Being well-informed

B Seeking information

C Providing information

D Collecting information

4 Cecilia thought that passing out flyers—

F wouldn't get people to take action

G wouldn't get support from her friends

H would require too much help from her mom

J would use too much paper and take too much time

GO ON

5 What does the word <u>supportive</u> mean in paragraph 4?

A   Creative

B   Encouraging

C   Patient

D   Youthful

6 What does the word <u>consequences</u> mean in section 6?

F   Pollutants

G   Results

H   Rewards

J   Warnings

7 Which words best describe Cecilia's attitude toward helping frogs?

A   Outraged and upset

B   Earnest and energetic

C   Interested and amused

D   Light-hearted and casual

8 What does the word <u>conditions</u> mean in section 6?

F   Situations

G   Illnesses

H   Problems

J   Worries

9 Under which subheading can readers find information about the correct depth for a frog pond?

A   Planning

B   Site Preparation

C   Planting

D   Caution

10 Which word BEST completes the sentence below?

The instructions direct kids to have their parents _____ them about where to make a pond.

F   advice

G   advise

H   adjust

J   affect

11 Look at the word <u>tadpoles</u> in paragraph 17. Then complete this analogy: <u>Full sun</u> is to <u>tadpoles</u> as <u>dry air</u> is to—

A   birds

B   fish

C   insects

D   plants

12 Cecilia's pond is most likely to become dirty and stagnant if she—

F   uses too few plants

G   makes the pond too wide

H   buys frogs to add to her pond

J   slopes the sides of the pond

GO ON

13 Based on information in the instructions, the reader can conclude that a pond will only help increase the local frog population if it—

A attracts frogs right away

B has more water lilies than grass

C is located in an area with full sun

D includes a shallow area with plants

14 Both the story and the instructions include information about—

F the correct depth for a frog pond

G threats to the survival of frogs

H habitat requirements of tadpoles

J organizing a pond-building class

15 Which word has the same sound as the underlined letters in uni**que**?

A guessing

B juicy

C league

D carnival

16 What does the word <u>impatient</u> mean?

F Very patient

G With a pat

H Patented

J Not patient

17 Which word correctly completes the sentence below?

Spreading a layer of sand is the step that _____ installing the pond liner.

A precedes

B presides

C proceeds

D processes

GO ON

> **Read this selection. Then answer the questions that follow it.**
> **Mark your answers on the Answer Document.**

Dreams for Sale

1   When a carpenter noticed a bit of yellow metal in a river in California, he started a wild chapter in American history. The year was 1848. The carpenter, a man named James Marshall, was building a mill for John Sutter along the American River. While working, Marshall's crew found gold by merely scratching the riverbank with a knife! Elated at their good fortune, they spread the word that there was a wealth of gold at Sutter's Mill. At first, most people regarded the claims as empty rumors. <u>Eventually</u>, a few tried their luck and returned with plump pouches of gold. Once people saw proof that the claims were true, word spread quickly. The city of San Francisco practically emptied out and closed down as its citizens invaded the Sutter's Mill area with picks and shovels in hand. The Gold Rush had begun!

2   While people all along the west coast were leaving their homes to look for gold, those back East received the news <u>warily</u>. It wasn't until a government worker published an official report and sent a boxful of

gold to Washington that gold fever spread through the whole country. People abandoned all feelings of caution once they learned the claims were proven. In their rush to strike it rich, people began to believe anything and everything they were told. After all, if there was proof that gold was floating in the rivers and lying on the ground all over California, anything might be true!

3   Many trusting people became <u>victims</u> of scam artists. Dishonest merchants took advantage of people's hopeful thinking. They made wild claims and false promises. Some guaranteed a quick and luxurious passage to the gold fields by carriage, ship, or wagon. One man claimed he had invented a flying machine that could repel bow and arrow attacks. He promised to get travelers to California in three days. In truth, there was no flying machine and almost all journeys to California were long, difficult, and dangerous.

4   Some merchants raised their prices for tools, guns, and anything else miners might buy. They got customers to spend money on useless gadgets by claiming that they were necessary for mining gold. One merchant even advertised a miraculous grease. It came with the promise that when rubbed onto the skin it would attract gold dust and make it stick to a miner's body!

5   Other people made a profit by selling information. They gave phony tips about the trip west or about gold-mining. They portrayed themselves as experts and sold books, maps, and tickets to lectures. Many of these so-called experts hadn't even been to California! In spite of their greedy <u>motives</u>, they always drew a crowd. They were masters at telling people what they wanted to hear. One speaker promised to reveal the <u>sites</u> of secret gold mines. Another declared that miners could make a thousand dollars a day. He insisted they could <u>extract</u> a half an ounce of gold from just one handful of dirt. One <u>mythmaker</u> claimed he had found huge chunks of pure gold. He described one as being the width of both his hands put together! As <u>improbable</u> as these tales were, gold-hungry crowds readily believed them. Most of the Gold Rush guidebooks made their authors rich while misleading those who read them.

6   Posters similar to the ones on the following pages <u>publicized</u> services for would-be gold miners. The ads were written to appeal to people's dreams of finding an easy fortune in the West.

Poster 1

CALIFORNIA BOUND!
Ride the *Silver Stage*
Take the Easy Road to Fortune!

Having outfitted this coach to suit the most discriminating traveler,

Silver Stage Travel Co.

is now offering comfortable passage to the richest gold fields in California.

Will depart the 3rd of March with luxurious accommodations and meals for the lucky travelers who are first to book passage.

Good-natured, experienced drivers devote every attention to your comfort and safety.

Explore the frontier in worry-free comfort while your parlor on wheels transports you over smooth, safe roads.

For further particulars, see
Martin D. Crawford, Agent

Poster 2

Richest Mines
in

CALIFORNIA!!
Gold Mining Secrets
will be revealed by
J. D. Morse
A foremost expert on locating gold in California

Mr. Morse, who has experienced firsthand the discovery of large lumps of pure gold ore, will deliver a

LECTURE
At 7 in the evening in the Town Hall
on the 5th day of April, 1849.

FORTUNE
awaits those who follow the instructions and advice of this well-informed guide. Your speaker will share his personal success story. Only he can provide the reliable information you have been seeking. He will recommend the best routes, camps, and mining destinations. As well, he will offer advice on provisions and gear. For a small fee, your speaker will furnish you with a map that shows the location of rich, but unexploited

SECRET MINES!!

18 In paragraph 1, the word <u>eventually</u> means—

F eagerly

G nervously

H right away

J after a while

19 What is the main idea of paragraph 2?

A Gold was lying on the ground all over California.

B Easterners were more cautious than Westerners.

C A government report caused gold fever to spread.

D People joined the Gold Rush without hearing any reports.

20 What does the word <u>warily</u> mean in paragraph 2?

F In a hopeful way

G In a cautious way

H In an astonished way

J In a disinterested way

21 What does the word <u>victims</u> mean in paragraph 3?

A People who are helped

B People who are tricked

C People who bother

D People who study

22 What information might have persuaded people to buy one merchant's miraculous grease?

F A promise that the grease would attract gold dust

G The grease's ability to repel bow and arrow attacks

H A promise that the grease would make people fly

J The grease's ability to help people travel faster

23 What does the word <u>motives</u> mean in paragraph 5?

A Feelings

B Reputations

C Profits

D Purposes

24 Based on the selection, the reader can conclude that many scam artists got rich during the Gold Rush because there was a—

F large supply of gold, but no way to get to it

G great desire for odd gadgets, but very few suppliers

H large number of newly rich miners, but not much to buy

J great demand for information, but not many facts available

GO ON

25 Information in the passage supports the generalization that the promise of wealth—

    A is always a false promise

    B only appeals to foolish people

    C helps most people find happiness

    D can cause people to use poor judgment

26 Which statement expresses the false promise that some Gold Rush guidebook authors hoped their readers would believe?

    F "For a small fee, I will sell you a book and a map."

    G "For a small amount of money, I will make you rich."

    H "For a few minutes of your time, I will entertain you."

    J "For a share of your profits later, I will give you free advice."

27 Which word is a homophone for the word <u>sites</u> in paragraph 5?

    A Sits

    B Kites

    C Cities

    D Sights

28 What does the word <u>publicized</u> mean in paragraph 6?

    F Surprised the public

    G Questioned the public

    H Made known to the public

    J Took money from the public

29 What does the word <u>transports</u> mean in Poster 1?

    A Carries

    B Leads

    C Pushes

    D Shows

30 In Poster 1, how do interested customers get prices for the Silver Stage service?

    F Wait for March 3

    G Contact the agent listed

    H Speak with the driver of the coach

    J Look for the correct stagecoach in town

31 Which feature of Poster 2 helps the reader know what kind of information audiences can expect to hear?

    A The name of the lecturer is near the top of the ad.

    B The word *lecture* is in larger type than other words.

    C Words related to getting rich are in capitalized letters.

    D The time and location are right below the word *lecture*.

32 Which does the word <u>extract</u> mean?

    F To write about

    G To put in

    H To create for

    J To pull out

GO ON

33 Which does the word <u>mythmaker</u> mean?

   A   A person who creates stories

   B   A person who likes nature

   C   A person who studies cultures

   D   A person from the past

34 What does the word <u>improbable</u> mean?

   F   Most probable

   G   Not probable

   H   Tending to babble

   J   Not very able

35 Which word correctly completes the sentence below?

Scam artists caused a lot of trusting people to _____ their money.

   A   loose

   B   lose

   C   lost

   D   loss

BE SURE TO MARK YOUR ANSWERS ON THE ANSWER DOCUMENT.

Writing: Revising and Editing

> **Read the introduction and the passage that follows it. Then read each question. Mark your answers on the Answer Document.**

On his computer, Michael typed this description of the bird-friendly back yard he and his family created. He wants you to help him correct it. As you read Michael's description, think about the changes he should make to correct and improve it. Then answer the questions that follow.

My Bird Paradise

(1) Last summer my dad suggested that, "We transform our backyard into an inviting place for birds." (2) Dad and I got helpful information from a book called Building a Bird Paradise. (3) We followed the author's instructions. (4) We planted trees and shrubs that produce berries and nuts. (5) Then we hung feeders near trees so birds could hide if they felt they were in danger. (6) We also put out two birdbaths so our visitors could drink without being crowded. (7) Last, we put a bell on our cat.

(8) That way the birds could hear him coming.

(9) I clean and refill the birdbaths every day so standing water won't cause a mosqeto problem. (10) My parents clean and fill the feeders.

(11) Dad's in charge of the feeders that hold seeds and Mom puts food in the hummingbird feeders.

(12) Now we spend most evenings on the back porch, watching birds. (13) It's a challenge to try to identify the bird sounds we hear. (14) At first I wasn't familiar with any of the birdcalls, but I'm slowly getting better at identifying them. (15) Now I always recognize the soft, cooing sound of a dove, the cheerful whistling sound of a cardinal, and the shrill screaming sound of a blue jay. (16) Someday I hope I can identify every bird that visits our backyard paradise.

---

1 What is the BEST way to revise sentence 1?

A Last summer, my dad suggested, "We transform our backyard into an inviting place for birds."

B Last summer, my dad suggested that we transform our backyard into an inviting place for birds.

C Last summer, my dad suggested that. We transform our backyard into an inviting place for birds.

D Last summer, my dad suggested, "That we transform our backyard into an inviting place for birds."

2 What change should be made in sentence 2?

F Change *I* to **me**

G Change *got* to **gotten**

H Insert a comma after **book**

J Type in italics ***Building a Bird Paradise***

GO ON

Name _____ Date _____

3 Which sentence could BEST be added before sentence 9?

 A Mom recognizes more bird calls than Dad and I do.

 B Mom, Dad, and I all work to maintain our bird-friendly yard.

 C I never knew that bird-watching could be so much fun.

 D We don't want insects to overtake the paradise we created.

4 What change should be made in sentence 9?

 F Change *refill* to **refills**

 G Insert a comma after *day*

 H Change *won't* to **didn't**

 J Change *mosqeto* to **mosquito**

5 What change, if any, should be made in sentence 11?

 A Change *Dad's* to **Dads**

 B Change *hold* to **holds**

 C Insert a comma after *seeds*

 D Change *Mom* to **mom**

6 What change should be made in sentence 14?

 F Change *At* to **In**

 G Insert a comma after *first*

 H Change *familiar* to **familiur**

 J Change *slowly* to **slow**

7 What is the BEST way to revise sentence 15?

 A Now I always recognize the soft cooing sound, of a dove, the cheerful whistling sound, of a cardinal, and the shrill screaming sound, of a blue jay.

 B Now I always recognize the soft, cooing sound of a dove; the cheerful, whistling sound of a cardinal; and the shrill, screaming of a blue jay.

 C Now I always recognize the soft, cooing, sound of a dove: the cheerful, whistling sound, of a cardinal: and the shrill, screaming sound, of a blue jay.

 D Now I always recognize the soft; cooing sound of a dove, the cheerful; whistling sound of a cardinal, and the shrill screaming sound of a blue jay.

GO ON

> **Read the introduction and the passage that follows it. Then read each question. Mark your answers on the Answer Document.**

Katy wrote this version of her favorite Native American legend. She would like you to read her story and suggest corrections and improvements she should make. When you finish reading, answer the questions that follow.

My Favorite Legend

(1) My grandmother, the greatest storyteller I know told me the following legend. (2) It comes from the mytholegy of the Papago people. (3) The story may have other names, but Grandmother calls it When Butterflies Were Born.

(4) One late summer's day, the Creator was enjoying the beautiful world he had made. (5) He smiled with satisfaction at the brilliant blue of the sky and the colorful clothing of children who were playing in the sunshine. (6) Nearby, the mothers of the children were grinding corn to store for the winter. (7) The lovely whiteness of the cornmeal brought another smile of contentment to the Creator's face. (8) Most delightful of all were the much bright colors of the summer flowers in the gardens all around.

(9) As the Creator thought about the coming change in the seasons, tears sprang to his eyes, for he realized that the sky would soon fade from blue to gray, and the children would put on their dull-colored coats. (10) The lovely white cornmeal would be hidden away in jars and the flowers would wither from their stems.

(11) Suddenly, the Creator was struck by a wonderful idea. (12) I will preserve all the vibrant colors of this day, he exclaimed, so that they will never fade from memory!

(13) He collected flowers of yellow, orange, purple, and crimson and put them in a bag. (14) Next he mixed in blue from the sky, white from the cornmeal and all the playful colors from the children's clothing. (15) Finally, he offered his new creation to the children, who eagerly opened the bag. (16) To everyone's delight, amazing colors flew out and seemed to float on the air. (17) This is how the first butterflies were born!

GO ON

8 What change, if any, should be made in sentence 1?

   F Change *grandmother* to **Grandmother**

   G Insert a comma after *know*

   H Change *legend* to **Legend**

   J Make no change

9 What change should be made in sentence 2?

   A Change *comes* to **come**

   B Change *mythelogy* to **mythology**

   C Change *Papago* to **papago**

   D Change the period to a question mark

10 What is the BEST way to revise sentence 3?

   F The story may have other names but Grandmother calls "it When Butterflies Were Born".

   G The story may have other names, but Grandmother calls it <u>When Butterflies Were Born</u>.

   H The story may have other names, but Grandmother calls it "When Butterflies Were Born."

   J The story may have other names, but Grandmother calls it 'When Butterflies Were Born.'

11 What change should be made in sentence 8?

   A Change *Most* to **More**

   B Change *delightful* to **delight**

   C Change *were* to **was**

   D Change *much bright* to **brilliant**

12 What change should be made in sentence 10?

   F Change *would* to **wood**

   G Change *hidden* to **hided**

   H Insert a comma after *jars*

   J Change *and* to **but**

13 What is the BEST way to revise sentence 12?

   A "I will preserve all the vibrant colors of this day, he exclaimed, so that they will never fade from memory!"

   B "I will preserve all the vibrant colors of this day," he exclaimed, "so that they will never fade from memory!"

   C "I will preserve all the vibrant colors of this day." He exclaimed, "so that they will never fade from memory!"

   D "I will preserve all the vibrant colors of this day" he exclaimed "so that they will never fade from memory!"

14 What change should be made in sentence 14?

   F Change *blue* to **blew**

   G Insert a comma after *cornmeal*

   H Change *playful* to **playfull**

   J Change *children's* to **childrens'**

GO ON

*On his computer, Don typed a book report about a mystery story that he read.
He would like you to read his first draft and suggest ways he can revise and
improve it. When you finish reading, answer the questions that follow.*

A Mystery with a Twist

(1) The Case of the Creepy Garage is the fifth book in the Freddy
Franklin mystery series. (2) In this latest book, a mysterious man and his
wife who move in next door arouse Freddy's suspicions.

(3) Day after day, bumping sounds wake Freddy before sunrise, but all
he can see is an eerie light flashing in the neighbors' garage. (4) The young
sleuth, hoping to expoze a brilliant crime, starts taking notes. (5) He
carefully observes the pre-dawn activities of his neighbor, or Dr Darkness,
as Freddy begins to call him. (6) After sunrise, the man leaves his house
in a truck, with a tarp over a large load in the back. (7) When he returns
the truck is always empty. (8) Meanwhile, the man's wife never appears
and her red car never leaves the driveway. (9) Freddy tries to convince his
parents that something illegal is going on but they dismiss his far-fetched
theories about a smuggling ring.

(10) The climax occurs early one morning when the neighbors leave in a rush. (11) They throw a suitcase into the red car and speed away, leaving the garage door wide open. (12) Freddy insists that they are headed to Las Vegas Nevada, with a suitcase full of loot. (13) His exasperated dad asks what will it take to convince you that you're imagining all this?

(14) When Freddy pleads for just one look inside the open garage, his dad reluctantly agrees. (15) When they peer in the garage, they see thousands of worms writhing and squirming in the back of the truck!

(16) I won't explain everything, but I'll give you three clues. (17) Some people raise earthworms to sell, earthworms will do anything to stay out of the light, and people hurry when a baby is on the way!

(18) This is the first book in which Freddy is wrong, and I really liked the unexpected ending. (19) I like mysteries by other authors, too. (20) Freddy I can't wait to read your next mystery! (21) Maybe you'll learn to go over and meet your new neighbors!

GO ON

15 What change should be made in sentence 1?

   A Type in italics *The Case of the Creepy Garage*

   B Change *fifth* to **five**

   C Change *Franklin* to **franklin**

   D Change *series* to **serious**

16 What change should be made in sentence 4?

   F Change *hoping* to **hopes**

   G Change *expoze* to **expose**

   H Change *starts* to **start**

   J Change *taking* to **taken**

17 What change should be made in sentence 5?

   A Change *carefully* to **careful**

   B Change *activities* to **activitys**

   C Insert a period after *Dr*

   D Change *him* to **he**

18 What change should be made in sentence 12?

   F Change *insists* to **insisted**

   G Insert a comma after *Las Vegas*

   H Change *Nevada* to **nevada**

   J Change *of* to **in**

19 What is the BEST way to revise sentence 13?

   A His exasperated dad asks, "What will it take to convince you that you're imagining all this"?

   B His exasperated dad "asks What will it take to convince you that you're imagining all this"?

   C His exasperated dad asks: What will it take to convince you that "you're imagining all this?"

   D His exasperated dad asks, "What will it take to convince you that you're imagining all this?"

20 What change should be made in sentence 20?

   F Insert a comma after *Freddy*

   G Change *can't* to **ca'nt**

   H Change *wait* to **weight**

   J Change *your* to **you're**

21 Which sentence does NOT belong in this paper?

   A Sentence 3

   B Sentence 7

   C Sentence 14

   D Sentence 19

GO ON ➡

Read the introduction and the passage that follows it. Then read each question. Mark your answers on the Answer Document.

Ana is writing a research report on the Dust Bowl. She would like you to read her first draft and suggest ways she can revise and improve it. When you finish reading, answer the questions that follow.

Dark Days of the Dust Bowl

(1) In 1930, a drought began in the United States and spread slowly across the central part of the country. (2) By 1934, it had turned America's grassy lands into a dessert. (3) Along with poor farming methods, this brought on the really super bad years of the Dust Bowl.

(4) It wasn't until 1935 that the driest part of the country got the name "Dust Bowl." (5) Robert Geiger, a reporter who traveled through the area, first used the term. (6) The Dust Bowl included these areas western Kansas, southeastern Colorado, the Oklahoma Panhandle, the Texas Panhandle, and northeastern New Mexico. (7) Another reporter who toured the Dust Bowl wrote, it is the saddest land I have ever seen.

(8) The Dust Bowl was especially difficult for those who lived on farms that disappeared under a blanket of dust. (9) Their life was made miserable by intense dust storms black blizzards that turned sunny days

GO ON

into complete darkness. (10) The dust buried tractors and cars. (11) It blew in through every door, window, and crack in a house.

(12) Seventy years later, those who survived the Dust Bowl remember those days clearly. (13) Their memmoirs are filled with details that sound like science fiction. (14) In an article entitled Dust Bowl Stories," one person described tying a towel over her nose and mouth every day to keep from getting sick. (15) Once, when caught in a storm, she covered her whole head and hung onto a fence to keep from blowing away!

(16) Though the drought years of the Dust Bowl ended around 1941, memories of those difficult days have not faded.

---

22 What change should be made in sentence 2?

F Change *turned* to **turn**

G Change *America's* to **america's**

H Change *grassy* to **grassly**

J Change *dessert* to **desert**

23 What change, if any, should be made in sentence 3?

A Change the comma to a colon

B Change *brought* to **bring**

C Change *really super bad* to **terrible**

D Make no change

24 What change should be made in sentence 6?

F Change *included* to **include**

G Insert a colon after *areas*

H Change *and* to **or**

J Change *New* to **new**

GO ON

25 What is the BEST way to revise sentence 7?

   A Another reporter who toured the Dust Bowl wrote. It is the saddest land I have ever seen.

   B Another reporter who toured the Dust Bowl wrote "It is the saddest land I have ever seen."

   C Another reporter who toured the Dust Bowl wrote It is the saddest land I have ever seen.

   D Another reporter who toured the Dust Bowl wrote, "It is the saddest land I have ever seen."

26 What change should be made in sentence 9?

   F Change *Their* to **There**

   G Change *miserable* to **miserible**

   H Insert parentheses around ***black blizzards***

   J Change the period to a question mark

27 What change should be made in sentence 13?

   A Change ***memmoirs*** to **memoirs**

   B Change *are* to **is**

   C Change *like* to **as if**

   D Change *fiction* to **fictional**

28 What change should be made in sentence 14?

   F Change *an* to **a**

   G Insert a quotation mark before ***Dust***

   H Change *tying* to **tieing**

   J Change *getting* to **get**

BE SURE TO MARK YOUR ANSWERS ON THE ANSWER DOCUMENT. STOP

Writing: Written Composition

Write about one specific way to make the world a better place. Choose <u>two</u> of the following genres that will best help you tell about your topic: nonfiction, fiction, poetry, journal entry, drama, public service announcement, or letter.

Use a separate sheet of paper to plan your composition. Then write your composition on the lined pages that follow.

The information in the box below will help you remember what you should think about when you write.

REMEMBER—YOU SHOULD

❏ choose <u>two</u> different genres that will best help you write about one topic

❏ for each genre you choose, include details that suit that genre

❏ present different ideas about the same topic in each genre

❏ use exact details to support your main ideas

❏ try to use correct spelling, capitalization, punctuation, grammar, and sentences

Name _____ Date _____

_____

_____

_____

_____

_____

_____

_____

_____

_____

_____

_____

_____

_____

_____

_____

Name _____ Date _____

Esperanza Rising

**Think back to the novel *Esperanza Rising* to answer questions 1–10.
Fill in the correct answers on the Answer Document.**

---

1 The setting of the beginning of the novel is—

A a camp cabin in Arvin, California

B a farm in Los Angeles, California

C a large ranch in Aguascalientes, Mexico

D at the border between Mexico and the United States

2 Who are the main characters in the novel?

F Marisol and Abuelita

G Isabel and Josephina

H Esperanza and Miguel

J Tío Luis and Tío Marco

3 When Esperanza and Miguel are described as being "on opposite sides of a deep river," it means—

A Miguel is 16 years old and Esperanza is only 13 years old

B Miguel is more privileged because he knows how to fix things on the ranch

C Esperanza is wealthy and of a higher class than Miguel, who is a servant's son

D Esperanza lives on a ranch on one side of the river and Miguel lives on the other side

4 Which characters create an obstacle for Esperanza?

F Miguel and Marta

G Ramona and Abuelita

H Hortensia and Alfonso

J Tío Luis and Tío Marco

5 Which of the following sentences best describes the conflict Esperanza and her mother face?

A Abuelita unraveled all of Esperanza's crocheted rows and made her start over.

B Esperanza pricked her finger on the thorn of a rose and Mama said it was bad luck.

C Esperanza's father died and Esperanza and her mother must flee to the United States.

D Esperanza's father died and she does not have the birthday party she would normally have had.

6 When Esperanza boards the train in Zacatecas, she is—

F eager but shy

G joyful and excited

H hopeful but afraid

J arrogant and rude

Name _____ Date _____

7 Marta is an important minor character in the novel because she—

   A likes Miguel and wants to take him away from Esperanza

   B is an American citizen and looks down on Mexican nationals

   C blindly follows the strikers without thinking of the welfare of her own mother

   D forces Esperanza to think about the lives and conditions of all migrant families and not just her own

8 After Esperanza's mother is hospitalized, Esperanza—

   F panics and asks Miguel to take her back to Aguascalientes to find Abuelita

   G joins Marta and the strikers to protest the low wages and squalor of the Mexican camps

   H knows she must think of herself to survive and not worry about her mother who is cared for by doctors and nurses

   J realizes she must become *la patrona*, responsible, and must work to pay the bills and bring Abuelita to her mother

9 The climax, or turning point of the novel, occurs when—

   A the immigration officials raid the camps and load strikers onto buses

   B Esperanza gives Isabel the doll to console her when she did not win Queen of the May

   C Miguel brings Abuelita to California and Tío Luis and Tío Marco no longer have control over their lives

   D Esperanza argues with Miguel because he agreed to dig ditches instead of confronting his boss at the railroad

10 A *proverb* is a familiar saying that is wise or contains a life lesson. Which of the following statements from the novel is not a proverb?

   F *Watch your fingers.*

   G *There is no rose without thorns.*

   H *He who falls today may rise tomorrow.*

   J *Wait a little while and the fruit will fall into your hand.*

BE SURE TO MARK YOUR ANSWERS ON THE ANSWER DOCUMENT.

Name _____ Date _____

Brian's Winter

> **Think back to the novel _Brian's Winter_ to answer questions 1–10.**
> **Fill in the correct answers on the Answer Document.**

1 Brian is alone in the Canadian wilderness because he—

A went on a hike and got lost

B wanted to run away from his family

C was in a plane crash and was marooned there

D was being tested on his survival skills by the Boy Scouts

2 Brian is relieved when the food rations in the survival kit are gone because—

F the freeze-dried food makes him sick

G the food rations do not include meat

H he doesn't like the taste of the food

J the food makes him think of home

3 Why is it best for Brian to boil meat in stew?

A Brian is afraid that flies will contaminate his food.

B Brian wants to make sure the meat is fully cooked.

C The nutrients from the meat will be retained in the broth.

D Boiling the meat in a stew will keep bears and wolves away.

4 What does Brian learn from observing the wolves?

F They run in packs.

G He learns to hunt.

H They are not afraid of him.

J They visit on a regular schedule.

5 Which of the following sentences does not support the idea that Brian is resourceful?

A He sews clothes of animal hides.

B He uses the cord in his sleeping bag to string his heavy bow.

C He misses the important warnings that summer is ending.

D He manages to seal and fortify the walls and doors of his shelter.

GO ON

Name _____ Date _____

6 The migrating geese are an important sign for Brian, because it means—

   F he will not be able to hunt geese

   G winter is coming and he must prepare

   H summer is coming and more food will be available

   J more rainy weather is in store and it will be difficult to hunt

7 After Betty sprays the bear, Brian is—

   A grateful to Betty for saving his life

   B hungry because he has no food left

   C angry because his shelter is damaged

   D making plans to hunt the bear with his bow and arrows

8 How does Brian feel about both the moose and the deer?

   F Fearful

   G Remorseful

   H Elated

   J Indifferent

9 What effect do the snowshoes have on Brian's outlook?

   A They enable him to stay at his camp more.

   B They boost his confidence in making clothing.

   C They give him more freedom outside the shelter.

   D They give him something to work on during a cold winter's night.

10 By the end of the novel, Brian is—

   F eager to return home to his family

   G reluctant to leave the wilderness he has come to enjoy

   H eager to fly in a plane after such a long time in the wilderness

   J reluctant to leave the Smallhorns because they have become his family

BE SURE TO MARK YOUR ANSWERS ON THE ANSWER DOCUMENT.

Tracking Trash: Flotsam, Jetsam, and the Science of Ocean Motion

---

**Think back to the novel *Tracking Trash* to answer questions 1–10.
Fill in the correct answers on the Answer Document.**

---

1 Which of the following statements is a fact?

A Franklin published the first map describing the so-called Gulf Stream in 1769.

B Dr. Ebbesmeyer's methods for understanding the ocean are, well, just a little unusual.

C Curt suspected that the toy-recovery pattern had something to do with the path the toys were following in the ocean.

D The warm waters of the Gulf Stream are believed to heat the winds that, in turn, carry a pleasant climate to northern Europe.

2 What initially caused a turn in Curt's career?

F His friend, Jim, showed him a computer program he had created.

G His mother showed him an article about the sneakers on beaches near Seattle.

H Captain Charles Moore found a floating patch of garbage and contacted Curt about it.

J Beachcombers contacted Curt about sneakers, toys, and hockey gloves they had found on beaches.

3 Which phrase summarizes the main idea of page 8?

A finding the location of the International Date Line

B sailors use maps with grids on them to find their way

C the ocean is divided into towns and streets, but there are few landmarks

D finding the exact location of the *Hansa Carrier* at the time of the sneaker spill

4 With which of the following statements is the author trying to persuade the reader to agree?

F Beachcombers play a vital role in scientific research.

G The OSCURS program is an important scientific tool.

H We all need to stop using disposable plastics in order to protect our oceans.

J The Eastern Garbage Patch is where currents have brought plastic trash from different locations.

Name _____ Date _____

5 Which of the following statements is not evidence for the dangers of plastic in our environment?

A Plastic is one of the most indestructible materials on the planet.

B Plastic is eaten by marine life such as sea turtles, jellyfish, and birds.

C Even the smallest pieces of plastic interact with contaminants in the ocean.

D Fish caught by commercial fishermen are contaminated when they eat contaminated jellyfish.

6 What evidence does the author give to support the statement that plastic is destroying one of Earth's most important natural resources?

F The author points out that plastic and contaminants can end up in our own food chain.

G Curt Ebbesmeyer thinks we cannot clean up the plastic in the Eastern Garbage Patch piece by piece.

H In 2005, Charlie and his team used a new type of trawl to analyze the amount of plastic below the sea's surface.

J The author explains that experiments that cannot be carried out in real life can be done with the OSCURS program.

7 Which of the following statements is an opinion?

A I think in our family of creatures we are misbehaving badly.

B Jim was a scientist at the National Oceanic and Atmospheric Administration.

C The *Hansa Carrier* was loaded to capacity when it collided with a vicious storm.

D OSCURS is a program that oceanographers use to fine-tune world surface current maps.

8 Ghost nets—

F are predators in the ocean

G are attached to fishing boats

H help the environment by catching trash

J endanger marine animals and destroy coral reefs

9 Dr. Mary Donohue's viewpoint on ghost nets is—

    A neutral

    B positive

    C negative

    D unbiased

10 The exact location of the Garbage Patch—

    F cannot be determined

    G changes from year to year

    H is found by beachcombers

    J is always in the same place

BE SURE TO MARK YOUR ANSWERS ON THE ANSWER DOCUMENT.